Would You Be
WILLING

AN INVITATION TOWARD WHOLENESS

Copyright 2019 by Mary Jo Graham

Published in Nashville, Tennessee by Hidden Crosses

All rights reserved. No part of this publication may be reproduced in any form, except for brief quotations in reviews, without the written permission of the author.

ISBN: 978-0-578-44023-1

Unless otherwise indicated, Scripture quotations are taken from The Holy Bible, New Living Translation R, C 1996, 2004, 2007, 2013 by Tyndale House Foundation. Used by permission of Tyndale House Publishers Inc., Carol Stream, Illinois 60188. All rights reserved.

Scripture quotations taken from the Amplified R Bible. C 1954, 1958, 1962, 1964, 1965, 1987 by The Lockman Foundation. Used by permission. Lockman.org.

Cover Design: Nathan Akers
Photography: Kristin Amaro - afH Capture & Design

Would You Be WILLING

AN INVITATION TOWARD WHOLENESS

MARY JO GRAHAM
AUTHOR OF *WHEN HE SENDS REDBIRDS*

Contents

Introduction 7

Section 1 — Would You Be Willing To Repent? 17
1: The Importance Of Repentance 21
2: Remind Me Again, Why Jesus? 29
3: The Joy Of Repentance. 37
4: Tough Love 45
5: Repentance vs. Worldly Sorrow. 55
6: Repenting For Our Nation 67

Section 2 — Would You Be Willing To Receive?. 77
7: Don't Stay Silent 81
8: Receiving Like A Child 89
9: Let's Start With The Basics - Forgiveness 95
10: You Are God's Favorite 103
11: Someone's Following You 111
12: VIP 121

Section 3 — Would You Be Willing To Reclaim? 131
13: You Have The Right To Reclaim 139
14: How Do You See It? 149
15: The Sword Of The Spirit 159
16: Get Off My Land! 169
17: Do It!... (You) / Do / It. 183
18: Falling In Love...Again 195

Section 4 — Would You Be Willing To Rejoice? 203
19: Fully Awake 209
20: "Shall We Dance?" 219
21: The Warfare Of Worship 227
22: Forever A Student 237
23: The Beautiful Body Of Christ 251
24: Shhhhhhh! 261

Section 5 — Would You Be Willing To Realign? 271
25: Pushing Off Or Pulling Up 275
26: He Works In The Waiting 291
27: The Need For Peeps 299
28: What Did You Say?...Sorry, I Was Distracted 309
29: Heavenly Repellant 317
30: Realignment Lightning Round 325

Section 6 — Would You Be Willing To Be Restored? 333
31: Bad Day For Pigs 339
32: When Jesus Stands 349
33: Choosing A God Path 361
34: He Called Me A "Woman" 373
35: Kissed By God 383
36: The Big Finale 393

Acknowledgements 401
Hidden Crosses Paintings 402
When He Sends Redbirds 403

Introduction

In May of 1982, I was looking forward to graduating from high school, then heading off to college. At that age, you tend to think you know everything and everyone over the age of say, forty, is either outdated or simple-minded. It's really that awkward age where you don't want anyone telling you what to do, yet you are clueless about how the world works.

Throughout most of my teenage years, and especially in high school, I tended to be a people-pleaser. The thought of someone being upset with me or misunderstanding my motives just made my heart race and my stomach nauseated. I just wanted to be liked and favored. I didn't really care about being popular or recognized, just liked by people in general. Of course, in those teen years there is always a lot of drama, no matter what time period you're from. For girls especially, you have a hard time knowing who you can trust with your heart. After all, it's so fragile and tender anyway, so the least little thing can feel like the world is crumbling around you. I knew there had to be something more…or maybe someone more.

From sixth grade through high school my closest friend was Lisa. To sum up our relationship was the word "laughter." Even to this day, over thirty-five years later, we still make each other laugh. Lisa and I would spend the night together often, and when we stayed at her house, I loved talking and visiting with her mother, Linda. Linda loved to laugh too, but more than anything, Linda loved Jesus.

Growing up I went to church, knew the main stories in the bible, could recite the Lord's Prayer, and took great pride in knowing many songs from the church hymnal. But Linda knew Jesus in a different way. She didn't just know Him… she LOVED Him! I can remember bible studies and prayer meetings taking place at Lisa's house. Although, Lisa and I would stay in her bedroom, I was always intrigued by what was happening down the hall. Sometimes Linda would be in the living room praying one-on-one with somebody in tears. She would boldly speak the name of Jesus over them and love them as though her hugs were from Christ Himself.

I didn't understand how this was happening in someone's home, instead of on Sunday morning at church, but there was something about this woman that was beyond herself.

For high school graduation, I received a letter from Linda. In this letter she encouraged me to seek the Lord and get to know Him. She told me she was praying for me and challenged me to pursue the life that God had already planned for me. This letter was her gift to me. At the time, I didn't understand nor appreciate this challenge and invitation. The scripture she included was Proverbs 3:5-6:

> *"Trust in the Lord with all your heart; do not depend on your own understanding. Seek His will in all you do, and He will show you which path to take."*
>
> PROVERBS 3:5-6

I remember folding up the letter and storing it with a box of pictures, newspaper clippings, and keepsakes. From graduation 1982 until about 1993, I pretty much led my life. I was "churched" but I lived my life on my terms, which translates to making selfish choices and sin choices. I guess you could say an average life, some good decisions and some really stupid decisions. I experienced times of joy and excitement, then times of disappointment and regret. The most frequent emotion I experienced was "confusion." Even after marrying a wonderful man, and having a beautiful daughter, I felt empty and without purpose.

In 1993, my husband and I decided to join a church, because we thought our three-year-old needed to be there! I love how God will let you believe what you want to believe, to get you where you need to be! In a small Sunday school classroom one Sunday morning, I finally "had ears to hear" the Gospel and realized my need for a relationship with Jesus. I was willing to lead my life in a different direction.

One night at 2 o'clock in the morning, I made the decision to repent of my sins, and totally give my life to Jesus. I was filled with the Holy Spirit and felt like a reset button had been pushed in my life. Before this time, I knew about God, understood religion, and thought life was about being a good person. I soon realized God didn't want my goodness, He wanted me! If I was willing to do things His way, then He had a better path. If I would trust Him and His ways, there would be purpose. Again, I was willing.

In today's culture, so many principles and character traits have been watered down. Even when we have desire to do a job or to help someone, there's a mediocre vibe, instead of a willingness for excellence. As I get older and continue to grow in my relationship with God, the word "willingness" has taken on new meaning. It's not just a "maybe" word, or a "unless I get a better offer" kind of word. Let's look at the words "willingness" and "willing" to get the full flavor of what it means:

Willingness—"the quality or state of being prepared to do something; readiness, promptitude, briskness, alertness, enthusiasm and joyousness."

Willing—"Inclined or favorably disposed in mind. Ready, willing and eager to help. Prompt to act or respond. Relating to the will or power of choosing, without reluctance. A willing sacrifice."

As I've reflected over these definitions, I certainly have been guilty of not showing promptness or enthusiasm in tasks where I've said I was willing to do them. My attitude was more reluctance for sure. Or my mind tried to figure out the minimum sacrifice, yet look like I'm giving maximum effort! Can you relate?

Also "willingness" and "desire" are NOT the same thing. Desire means, *"a strong feeling of wanting to have something or wishing for something to happen."* I have such a strong desire to lose 15lbs…yet I'm not willing to change my eating habits or exercise more. I desire to get up earlier in the mornings to spend more time with the Lord, yet not willing to set my alarm any earlier. Ouch, that one hurt a little! Desire is not a bad thing, in fact, it can help motivation. But willingness makes things happen!

In the last definition of "willing" it reminds me of someone who made a willing sacrifice. Someone who spoke such a profound prayer to God in Luke 22:42,

> *"Father, if you are willing, please take this cup of suffering away from me. Yet I want your will to be done, not mine."*
>
> LUKE 22:42

In other words, "I am willing to do things Your way!" Jesus actually <u>desired</u> an optional plan, but he clearly obeys the Father with "I AM <u>WILLING</u>!!!"

Thank you Jesus for Your willingness to carry out the perfect plan of Father God! Jesus' willingness to sacrifice His life on the cross for me and for you was not a picture of "dragging his feet" or "with reluctance." When he said "yes" to the cross it was with full mind, heart and yes, body. He was prompt and obedient out of trust in His Father's plan. Jesus was all in…all mind, all heart, all body. An attitude of willingness doesn't always know the path ahead, all the details, or what the response of others will be. Willingness says, "Let's do this God's way," trusting that He already holds the plan in His hand.

The most foundational act of our will is the decision to choose Jesus as Lord and Savior. It is an individual choice we are able to make, because God set it up that way. We have been given a free will to choose God. In fact, even after we have accepted the gift of salvation and are born again, we still have the free will to choose Jesus daily…His ways, His character, His thoughts and His will.

I try to be a transparent person, mainly because I've

realized my mistakes and bad choices could help others avoid the same ones. I also love sharing the Word of God and what you can learn from stories in scripture. Most of all, I love freedom! That feeling of peace, contentment and joy on the inside is priceless! Having victory on the inside, even if the outward circumstances haven't caught up yet with the God-plan.

When I experience and receive breakthroughs or spiritual truths from the Lord, I love to share them. Believers need to do that...share! Over the years, the Lord has taught me many things while praying with others and especially having others pray for me. I've learned more and more about the power of WILLINGNESS. For example, wanting to forgive someone, yet not being WILLING to let go of the anger. Or wanting to get to know God more, yet not being WILLING to read the Bible. Or maybe the struggle of wanting to just feel better about yourself, yet not be WILLING to let Jesus heal a past of shame or guilt. WILLINGNESS is huge and so important!

In this book, I share things I've learned about willingness, prayer, and cooperating with the Holy Spirit. I've found when I cooperate more fully with God, then I have greater peace and greater joy, while growing closer to Him. I have divided this book into six "willingness" sections, with six chapters in each section. These chapters are simply my personal stories, bible stories, and examples of how each "willingness" looks in everyday life...hopefully making it practical to apply and live out! Here are the sections:

> **Would You Be Willing To Repent?**
> **Would You Be Willing To Receive?**
> **Would You Be Willing To Reclaim?**
> **Would You Be Willing To Rejoice?**
> **Would You Be Willing To Realign?**
> **Would You Be Willing To Be Restored?**

Why these sections? What I have discovered in praying with people, and in my own life, is there is sometimes a misunderstanding about *repentance*. Or we might understand *repentance*, yet never understand how to *receive* forgiveness from God. Or we may understand *repentance* and *receiving*, but never realize the authority we have in Jesus to *reclaim* places in our mind and emotions that are tormented by our past. Or maybe we have been taught that *rejoicing* is what you do only in a church service. Or times we slowly fall back into old habits, but not realize we need to *realign* back with the truth of the Word of God. And finally, maybe believing we have to live with life the way it is...the "nothing will ever change" syndrome...no *restoration*. There is an order to this book, so I encourage you to simply take the chapters one at a time and allow them to build. Read a chapter...talk to the Lord...listen to Him.

At the end of most chapters are prayers. I encourage you to read each one out loud. Some chapters may just end in scripture...read out loud! Hearing ourselves pray and hearing the scripture spoken is powerful. Also, as you move from chapter to chapter, if a thought comes to mind, or maybe another scripture verse, write it down! Make personal notes or prayers.

I will also be referencing many scripture passages, so having a Bible in hand is recommended. The majority of my scripture references are from the New Living Translation. This book can also be used in a small group! Feel free to grab a couple of friends and go through this book together... praying and encouraging each other chapter by chapter!

I confess I am still learning about the Lord...learning more about His ways, learning to hear His voice, and learning to cooperate more fully with Him. In fact, now when I read Proverbs 3:5-6, it sounds more like this,

Would you be willing to trust Me with all your heart?

Would you be willing to not depend on your own understanding?

Would you be willing to seek My will in all you do?

Would you be willing to let Me show you which path to take?

Kind of puts the ball in our court, doesn't it? But, if we are willing....then the ball moves back into His court, which is the best place it can be!! Willingness is an invitation toward wholeness. Let's begin....

SECTION ONE

Would You Be Willing To Repent?

We will begin the first section with the topic of repentance. Repentance is an interesting word. It has such a sorrowful sound to it when you say it. Perhaps even has that "guilt and shame" kind of feeling. The kind where you hang your head low and maybe even fall to your knees with remorse. The meaning of the word is actually, "a sincere regret or remorse." Coming to the place of regret and remorse in your heart towards God is a good thing, yet in religious circles, it sometimes is viewed as coming before an angry God and hoping He will accept your sorrow and possibly let you have some kind of relationship with Him. Is this the correct picture of repentance? Or could it be a word that offers a visual of running to God with assurance that His arms are stretched out ready for a spiritual embrace? I should hope this visual is more appealing and can lead to a life of hope, freedom and change as we grow in relationship with an incredibly, loving Father.

Over the next six chapters let's look at what God is offering to us and also, what is our part in our relationship with Him. Remember, this IS a relationship…getting to know Him more and more. My prayer for you and for me is from the writings in 2 Peter 1:2-3,

> *"May God give you more and more grace and peace as you grow in your knowledge of God and Jesus our Lord. By his divine power, God has given us everything we need for living a godly life. We have received all of this by coming to know him, the one who called us to himself by means of his marvelous glory and excellence."*
>
> 2 PETER 1:2-3

Oh, make no mistake, He is a God of justice and He is mighty, yet He is a God of mercy and goodness. His love is everlasting and He is a God who can push a reset button in a life. Let's begin with the first "R" of this journey… Repentance. It is such a beautiful word!

CHAPTER ONE

The Importance Of Repentance

The first biblical character I think of when I hear the word **repentance** is John the Baptist. Can you imagine seeing this guy preaching in the wilderness and shouting at the top of his lungs?

> *"Repent of your sins and turn to God, for*
> *the Kingdom of Heaven is near!"*
>
> MATTHEW 3:2

This radical man, whose father was the priest, Zechariah, was on the priest path since birth. His destiny was to walk in the footsteps of his dad, wear the robe, go into the Holy of Holies and present before God the sins of the people. It was an important job and obviously a respected job. After all, John was like a preacher's kid, so everyone knew the path he was suppose to take. Yet this man, John, was different and he had a call on his life and it wasn't to be a priest in the traditional sense. His call was important, because it was a fulfillment of prophecy in the Old Testament,

> *"He is a voice shouting in the wilderness, Prepare the way for the Lord's coming! Clear the road for him!"*
>
> ISAIAH 40:3

This guy wore camel hair for clothes and ate locusts and wild honey…a far cry from a priest's wardrobe and diet. He didn't do his shouting in the temple or on the city streets. This man took his ministry into the wilderness! Frankly, it is where the majority of us truly meet the Lord…in the wilderness of our lives. We find ourselves stuck in a life of dryness, drought, and nothing is growing in us but weeds.

I read an article recently about a multimillionaire who was battling depression. What? Money, cars, houses, travel… you name it and he had it at his fingertips. Yet the soul of this man was in the desert…the wilderness. He was spiritually

The Importance Of Repentance

parched.

King Solomon experienced this and toward the end of his life penned his emotions in the Book of Ecclesiastes. This king of wisdom confessed he had denied himself no pleasure, whether it was physical, social, work, play, etc. Yet his soul cried out, "Empty!" So a wilderness life has nothing to do with bank accounts, education, intellect or social status. It's the state of the inside of a man or woman.

In order to be right with God and walk with Him, we have to belong TO Him. John gives us our part in walking with God in two steps, "<u>Repent</u> of your sins and <u>Turn</u> to God." We have to repent of our sins, which is simply confessing our sins and asking God to forgive us for living our life apart from Him. Visualize if you will, wandering around a desert alone, with no guidance, no provision, and no hope. That is living apart from God. It's a path of darkness and death. Since it doesn't hinge on your status in life, it is a spiritual state…a mental state. So to repent simply means to change your mind…to think differently. Without a change of mind, it is impossible to turn to God.

What does it mean to <u>turn</u> to God? Again, let's get a visual of this. I love weddings. I love the celebration and the love flowing from witnessing a bride and groom becoming husband and wife. There are two parts of a wedding I look forward to. One is the look on the groom's face when he sees his bride walking towards him. Priceless.

The second thing I anticipate is when the minister says, "Please turn and face each other." He then proceeds to lead them in saying their vows to one another. OK, have you ever been to a wedding where the bride and groom DON'T look at each other when they say their vows? Whether it's nerves or confusion, they end up looking at the minister during the repeating of the vows! How awkward! I just want to yell from the pew, "Hey, you are suppose to turn to each other and say your vows...you're not marrying the minister!"

My favorite wedding memories are my daughters' weddings. They both chose to recite their own vows to their husbands and vice versa. The way they looked at each other made my heart melt. Eyes locked, all smiles, some tears...in a room filled with guests, it was as if they were all alone... just the two of them, excited about starting a future together. That's "turning." This is what our relationship with God should look like. Turning to God, looking to Him and Him only. Then, us receiving the vows He made through the Cross of His Son, Jesus, and the blood He shed. Then, me looking at Him and saying, "I look to you Lord, I choose to follow and walk with You all the days of my life. I choose to give you my whole heart and cling to You!"

For those of you who are married, you know that just saying the vows on your wedding day, and sealing the deal with a public kiss...well, that is only the beginning of the marriage covenant. You are not just living for you; therefore you have to make various changes in your actions, speech, thoughts, motives, schedule, etc. ...you consider first your spouse. In your relationship with God, by repenting and turning to Him, change also occurs and you should expect it and desire it.

In Matthew 3:8-9, John the Baptist addresses the religious experts and priests by making a sobering statement right after he calls them unflattering names. These religious authorities claimed to know God, yet their lives said otherwise. In other words, their actions, attitudes, and hearts did not prove or reflect that they had a relationship with God. It was all for show and perks. John tells them,

> "<u>Prove by the way you live</u> that you have repented of your sins and turned to God. Don't just say to each other, 'We're safe, for we are descendants of Abraham.' That means nothing, for I tell you, God can create children of Abraham from these very stones."
>
> MATTHEW 3:8-9

The word "prove" means to "bring forth fruit." In the original Greek translation, the visual of this is bringing or bearing luscious, healthy fruit in our work, acts, deeds, profit, praises and how we thank God. It's also a "gathering" word which means when our lives change from repenting and turning to God, then our lives draw others to God as well.

Isn't that amazing?!

Each and every time we turn to God, we should expect change. We should expect and take steps of obedience to walk out the Word of God in the way we live our lives. Nothing about the Bible, about God, about Jesus or about life will ever make sense without repentance and turning to the One who offers Life... Because He is the giver of Life! He's the ONLY one who can breathe a new spiritual life in you! When you repent and turn to God through believing in the death and resurrection of Jesus Christ, you experience a birth into a new Kingdom! A new citizenship! Just like in marriage, where two are one and there is a taking on of a new name…so it is with accepting this amazing gift from God.

Walk toward Him down the aisle…see His face. That's the face of The Bridegroom…Jesus. He's calling in the wilderness…Come and be SAVED!

If you have never asked Jesus to be Lord in your life, I invite you to say this prayer out loud…

"Heavenly Father, I come to You and repent of my sins. I don't want to live apart from You or make decisions apart from You. Please forgive me Lord and help me to change. I choose to turn to You and only You. You are my source of life, strength, hope and love. Let my heart beat for You and help me to change in thoughts, words and actions. Help me turn to You daily. Fill the emptiness in my mind and

emotions, and breathe on the places of wilderness in my life. Reset my heart and teach me how to live for You. In the name of Jesus. AMEN."

> *"If you confess with your mouth that Jesus is Lord and believe in your heart that God raised him from the dead, you will be saved. For it is by believing in your heart that you are made right with God, and it is by confessing with your mouth that you are saved."*
>
> ROMANS 10:9-10

> *"This means that anyone who belongs to Christ has become a new person. The old life is gone; a new life has begun!"*
>
> 2 CORINTHIANS 5:17

> *"I preached first to those in Damascus, then in Jerusalem and throughout all Judea, and also to the Gentiles, that all must repent of their sins and turn to God—and prove they have changed by the good things they do.*
>
> ACTS 26:20

CHAPTER TWO

Remind Me Again, Why Jesus?

"I am the Way, the Truth and the Life. No one can come to the Father except through me."

JOHN 14:6

This statement from Jesus pretty much says it all. He is clearly saying that there is no possible way to get to God except through Him. Before Jesus made this mind-blowing statement to the disciples, Thomas had just asked him in confusion, "We have no idea where you are going, so how can we know the way?" We have all been "Thomas" in our lives.

Maybe before being born again, maybe after conversion, or even during our daily relationship with Jesus…at some point we want the assurance of "The Way." Jesus doesn't stutter when he says, "It's Me!"

Let's go back in time to this meeting of Jesus and the disciples. The disciples were Jewish men who believed in God. They understood about making animal sacrifices for the forgiveness of their sins. They understood religious festivals, keeping the Jewish laws and traditions, and all the do's and don'ts. They understood that a Messiah would come one day. Now this man tells them, "You are looking at Him!" And He goes so far as to explain, "If you have seen me, you have seen the Father." Like Father, Like Son.

Even today there is a struggle with seeing Jesus as the only way to God. As we said in Chapter 1, without repentance there is no understanding of God. We have to turn to Him. We have to walk to Him…the Way. For Jesus to tell these men and others that He was The Way meant one of two things; He was who He said He was or He was a liar.

I can tell you that I am the governor of Tennessee, but I would be lying, because that is not who I am. If I told multitudes of people this lie and ask them to follow me, I would not only be a liar, but a very bad person and maybe a little power hungry too! I have heard people say, "Well, I believe Jesus was a good man, but I believe there are many ways to God." A "good man" wouldn't lie and lead people astray by claiming He was God in the flesh.

I'd like to present three passages of scripture:

> "In the beginning the Word (Christ) already existed. The Word was with God and the Word was God. He existed in the beginning with God. God created everything through him and nothing was created except through him. The Word gave life to everything that was created, and his life brought light to everyone. "
>
> JOHN 1:1

> "Christ is the visible image of the invisible God. He existed before anything was created and is supreme over all creation, for through him God created everything in the heavenly realms and on earth. He made the things we can see and the things we can't see —such as thrones, kingdoms, rulers and authorities in the unseen world. Everything was created through him and for him. He existed before anything else, and he holds all creation together."
>
> COLOSSIANS 1:15-17

> "And now in these final days, he has spoken to us through his son. God promised everything to the Son as an inheritance, and through the Son he created the universe."
>
> HEBREW 1:2

The Disciple John, the Apostle Paul and the writer of Hebrews are telling us that "in the beginning" when God created all things, Jesus Christ was there…The Word. Nothing was created, but through Him…and for Him.

> *"Then God said, "Let us make human beings in our image, to be like us."*
>
> GENESIS 1:26

Us? Our? These words are plural. Father, Son and Holy Spirit. One God…three distinct roles. Three-in-one creating.

God creating through Jesus Christ (Life), and through the Holy Spirit (Power). It looks something like this:

God > through Jesus Christ (Life) > by Holy Spirit (power) > made Creation/Humans

Because of sin all the way back in the garden (read Genesis Chapter 3) we were separated from a Holy God. Therefore, it only makes sense that if we were created by God…through Jesus Christ... by the power of the Holy Spirit….THEN the only way to return to God is… through Jesus Christ… by the power of the Holy Spirit. It looks like this:

Me > by the power of the Holy Spirit > through Jesus Christ (Life) > God

> "For God in all his fullness was pleased to live in Christ and through him God reconciled <u>everything</u> to Himself. He made peace with everything in heaven and on earth by means of Christ's blood on the cross."
>
> COLOSSIANS 1:19-20

Jesus is not only the WAY; He has ALWAYS been the WAY. Everything was created through Him; therefore He is the only door to go back through to get to God....to Eternal Life. There is no Eternal Life except through THE LIFE.... Jesus Christ. He is the only one who IS God, and came down from heaven in human form. He is the only one God sent to die for our sins on a cross. He was the only one to be raised from the dead, so we could have eternal life. From Genesis to Revelation, all scriptures point to Jesus. He is the bridge. In John 1:51 Jesus said,

> "I tell you the truth, you will all see heaven open and the angels of God going up and down on the Son of Man, the one who is the stairway between heaven and earth."
>
> JOHN 1:51

Everyone sins. I recognize that I still sin. I don't want to, nor is it intentional (95% of the time!), but in this fleshly body I still battle with offense, anger, selfishness, pride...I think I'll stop there. I am flawed, but God has given me a gift. The gift of repentance. Living a life of repentance recognizes that it is only through Jesus that we are reconciled back to God. Therefore, it is ONLY through Jesus that I am changed! Repenting and turning to God changes the way I think, act, talk and see. I begin viewing life through His eyes...seeing a bigger picture. And through this amazing process comes the reality that I cannot fix myself and neither can you. I can do my part, which is obedience to cooperate with God's will and make the decision to change my ways, so this beautiful change can transform me.

> *"If we confess (or repent) our sins to Him,*
> *He is faithful and just to forgive us our sins*
> *and to cleanse us from all wickedness."*
>
> 1 JOHN 1:9

> *"My dear children, I am writing this to you so that you will not sin. But if anyone does sin, we have an advocate who pleads our case before the Father. He is Jesus Christ, the one who is truly righteous. He himself is the sacrifice that atones for our sins— and not only our sins, but the sins of all the world."*
>
> 1 JOHN 2:1-2

> *"Because God's children are human beings—made of*

> *flesh and blood — the Son also became flesh and blood. For only as human being could he die, and only by dying could he break the power of the devil, who had the power of death. Only in this way could he set free all who have lived their lives as slaves to the fear of dying."*
>
> HEBREW 2:14-15

Pray this prayer out loud with me,

"Heavenly Father, I repent and ask You to forgive me for doubting at any time that Jesus is the only Way. Thank You for sending Your Son to take my place so I could be forgiven and have eternal life. I rejoice that through the power of the Holy Spirit, I am reconciled to You and I am righteous before You, because of the blood Christ shed for me on the Cross. I ask You to cleanse me of offense, pride, selfish ways and anything that puts a wedge between You and me. Quicken in me daily, by Your Spirit, any area, any thoughts, or any actions that I need to repent and turn from. Teach me Your ways of reacting so that I can reflect Your character. Let my thoughts be Your thoughts and my ways be Your ways. Thank you for Your goodness and how much You love me.

In the name of Jesus. AMEN."

CHAPTER THREE

The Joy Of Repentance

Close your eyes and allow God to bring to mind a visual when I say these words:

Party...Clapping...Shouting

What did you see? I'll tell you what I see. I see a lot of people with smiles on their faces. I see streamers, lots of balloons, confetti, and food. I see people clapping, cheering and shouting to the point it is almost deafening. Well guess what? This is a humanized glimpse of heaven when we repent!

In the Gospel of Luke, Chapter 15 (read), Jesus tells three parables referring to being lost and then being found. Our story opens with Jesus socializing and having dinner with well-known sinners. Not just any ole sinners, but the worst of the worst…tax collectors. The religious priests could not believe Jesus would even associate with such a motley crew! I always love how Jesus puts "religious" people in their place.

This reminds me of a story my Daddy used to tell about my great-grandmother, Rhodie. She was a fiery little lady who attended a rather traditional church. One evening a meeting was held in the church to decide on whether or not to kick "Mr. Such-in-Such" out of the church. One after another, people spoke and agreed he needed to be voted out! Then Rhodie raised her frail hand and proceeded to stand before the church members. In a calm voice she spoke, "Well, I would just be afraid to vote someone out that the Lord wanted in." Meeting adjourned!

Responding to the Pharisees, Jesus first tells a story of a man who lost one of his sheep out of 100 sheep. And this sheep wasn't just lost; it was lost in the wilderness. We find Jesus most often rescues us in the wilderness. In the wilderness there is little food, limited water, wild animals and certain death. The owner leaves his flock of sheep to look for it, knowing it will die without his help. When he finds it, he carries it home on his shoulders. Not only does he carry it home, but he tells his friends and family to come over to celebrate! You may say, "Well, that's a new believer accepting Jesus."

We are all created by God and it is God's desire we all are "found" as lost sheep. So while that is very, very true, also consider this...the lost sheep was a part of a flock to begin with. The man knew the sheep was his and the sheep knew the master. They had a relationship already established.

The second story is about a woman who lost a coin. She had other coins, but she searched high and low to find one particular coin. When she found it, she too calls friends and family to celebrate. Again, this coin was a part of the ten coins she had at the beginning. It was already a part of a collection.

Finally, Jesus tells about two sons. Both sons had access to their father's money. One decided to take his inheritance and go do his own thing, make his own decisions and be in charge of his life. It didn't take long before he realized he had it pretty good with his father, and life separated from dad was horrible. As he approaches home, the father runs to him with arms open wide! The father doesn't preach, scold, or correct this foolish son, but rather he pours out compassion, hugs, kisses and unconditional love. He proceeds to throw the biggest party ever and celebrate this lost son coming home. Remember, this young man was already a son...a part of the family. The son had a relationship with his dad, called him dad, yet chose to stray from his dad.

In all three stories, Jesus describes the scene in heaven when a sinner repents...an all out celebration with angels singing full of joy! Jesus even says in verse 7 of Chapter 15,

> *"In the same way, there is more joy in heaven over one lost sinner who **repents and returns** to God than over ninety-nine others who are righteous and haven't strayed away."*
>
> LUKE 15:7

Therefore in this scenario, one can only **return** if one had relationship with God in the first place.

There is no doubt that 100% of the time heaven has the biggest celebration of all when an unbeliever turns to God. I love the lyrics from the song, *Amazing Grace*, *"once I was lost, but now I am found."* I'll always remember meeting Jesus for the first time and how His grace loved me to repentance and accepting Him as Lord and Savior. But since that memorable day, I confess I have a tendency to get a little "lost" again. Jesus hasn't moved…I have. Nevertheless, I have a Lord who comes after me with open arms and says, "Repent and turn!" I have a Shepherd who goes to great lengths to rescue me… time after time! I belong to Him!

Let's be honest…as Christians we get lost! How amazing to know Heaven rejoices when we repent yet again! When we turn to the King once more and humble ourselves to His Lordship! The beauty of repentance reminds us that no matter what…he still forgives and celebrates when we yield back to Him. Are there consequences to "straying" and making selfish decisions in our lives? Most definitely, yes! Does God absorb some of those consequences, because of His grace and mercy? Most definitely, yes! Do we need to cooperate more with changing our ways? Amen!!! Yet there is nothing like "coming home" and running back to the Father. So....

- No matter what you have done
- Where you have been
- How you backslid
- Thoughts you have had
- Choices you have made
- Wrong words you have spoken
- Pride
- Judgment
- Gossip
- Etc
- Etc

Repent! Turn! Be willing to change! The Father is waiting, and He wants to run to you with open arms. He misses you! Let the Holy Spirit show you daily if there are things you need to repent of and areas that need to change. Don't put it off! Don't let anything come between you and your fellowship with Jesus. Repent! It brings a smile to God's face, because it is another step in changing us to look and act more like Him...and it keeps a party going in heaven!

> *"I will praise the Lord at all times. I will constantly speak his praises. I will boast only in the Lord; let all who are helpless take heart. Come, let us tell of the Lord's greatness; let us exalt his name together. I prayed to the Lord, and he answered me. He freed me from all my fears. Those who look to him for help will be radiant with joy; no shadow of shame will darken their faces. In my desperation I prayed, and the Lord listened; he saved me from all my troubles. For the angel of the Lord is a guard; he surrounds and defends all who fear Him. Taste and see that the Lord is good. Oh, the joys of those who take refuge in him!"*
>
> PSALM 34:1-8

"Heavenly Father, I want to make You smile daily. Since You are always ready to receive me with opened arms, I ask You to help me run to You daily. Help me Lord, to never hesitate in bringing You my flaws, bad habits or stubborn ways. I desire change Lord, and I am willing to yield to Your ways. You know me through and through, therefore each day I have a welcomed invitation to turn to You. Cleanse me…in my thoughts, choices and words, so Your light can shine through me. As I look to You, let Your ways become my ways and let my reflection look more and more like You.

In the name of Jesus. AMEN"

CHAPTER FOUR

Tough Love

One of the greatest verses of a heart crying out in repentance is from King David. This man of God, who loved God with all his heart, chose to make some life altering decisions. He committed adultery and murder. This was actually a common practice for kings, but this was not just any king. This was a king who grew up serving God, trusting God, worshipping God and loving God. This man was God's choice as King of Israel.

Have you ever experienced God's love in the form of Him sending you someone to say, "Hey, you are in sin and God is saying, 'Stop It!'" That is not just "calling you on the carpet"… that is great love! In fact, for God to do this shows just how jealous He is for us. He loved David so much He sent the prophet, Nathan, to tell David, "Enough!" David responds in Psalm 51:1-2 with the proof of God's great love,

> *"Have mercy on me God, because of your unfailing love. Because of your great compassion, blot out the stain of my sins. Wash me clean from my guilt. Purify me from my sin."*
>
> PSALM 51:1-2

David knew God's forgiveness was available for one reason and one reason only…God's extraordinary love and compassion for him. David knew his sin was rooted in rebellion. He also knew his sin was tearing him apart. His joy was gone and he was losing sleep, night after night. He also knew he couldn't fix the mess he had made. The sin had gotten so heavy it was emotionally and mentally paralyzing him.

Have you ever felt like sin was paralyzing you? Perhaps it is a sin that has lingered so long that you didn't think it was possible to approach God. Or maybe you could fix it or change it before you even spoke to God about it. At the time, this kind of thinking seems to make sense, but it is crazy to think we can forgive our own sin, fix our sin, or hide our sin. All we are doing is driving a bigger and bigger wedge between us and a loving Father.

When we belong to God, it is through HIS faithfulness that He does everything possible to rescue us. Even when we are not faithful, He remains true to Himself. He doesn't leave us or forsake us. He will prompt others to come check on us, encourage us, love us….even convict us. Wow, what a friend!

Also, what happens when God chooses you to be this kind of friend to someone else? Well…it isn't easy. There is a risk of losing a friend, or at the least starting a disagreement. For Nathan the prophet to approach the King of Israel and share his insight was risking his very life. Yet Nathan knew he had to please and obey God.

As the King of Israel, no one would have questioned David's actions or reputation. So the opinions of others did not matter…what mattered was David was tormented on the inside. Sin will do that you know…Torment. It also makes us feel dirty…unclean. We desperately need to be purified. Sexual sin, immorality and greed will steal a purified heart. Why? Because it causes guilt and shame. It separates us from God. David's words spell this out perfectly in verses 7-11 of Psalm 51,

> *"Purify me from my sins, and I will be clean; wash me, and I will be whiter than snow. Oh, give me back my joy again; you have broken me—now let me rejoice. Don't keep looking at my sins. Remove the stain of*

my guilt. Create in me a clean heart, O God. Renew a loyal spirit within me. Do not banish me from your presence, and don't take your Holy Spirit from me."

PSALM 51:7-11

This world is in a sexual nightmare; in fact, sin is at our fingertips. We live in a computerized world with laptops and mobile devices in our hands constantly. It takes effort, discipline, and watchfulness to avoid sexual sin in thought and action. We have to choose to diligently run from the lures of sexual invitations that the enemy offers. The Apostle Paul was very clear how we should view and act toward sexual sins. Here are just a few scriptures:

"Run from sexual sin! No other sin so clearly affects the body as this one does. For sexual immorality is a sin against your own body."

1 CORINTHIAN 6: 18

"Let there be no sexual immorality, impurity, or greed among you. Such sins have no place among God's people. Obscene stories, foolish talk, and coarse jokes—these are not for you. Instead, let there be thankfulness to God. You can be sure that no immoral, impure or greedy person will inherit the Kingdom of Christ and of God. For a greedy

person is an idolater, worshiping the things of this world."

EPHESIANS 5:3-5

"So put to death the sinful, earthly things lurking within you. Have nothing to do with sexual immorality, impurity, lust, and evil desires. Don't be greedy, for greedy person is an idolater, worshiping the things of this world."

COLOSSIANS 3:5

"Run from anything that stimulates youthful lusts. Instead, pursue righteous living, faithfulness, love, and peace. Enjoy the companionship of those who call on the Lord with pure hearts."

2 TIMOTHY 2:22

Notice that Paul uses the word, "Run!" or in some translations, "Flee!" Do you know what this word means in the original Greek language? Not a trick question...it means FLEE! The visual is **"turning and running away as fast as possible to safety, because there is a crucial need to escape danger or a potential vice!"** Wow! This kind of sin is so damaging to us, our relationships and especially with our walk with God, that He says "RUN!" In other words, treat sexual sins like a deadly poison.

It is interesting that Paul frequently combines sexual immorality and impurities with the word greed. When we think of the word greed, we first think in terms of money. But greed is anything we think we have to have to satisfy our selfish desires. King David watched Bathsheba with lustful eyes and chose to give in to his greedy feeling that said, "I have to have her!" He ignored the fact that she was married...to one of his mighty warriors, I might add. This sin snowballed to the point he had this faithful soldier killed just to cover his sin. But sin can't be covered or hidden....only confessed and cleansed.

For Christ-Followers, Jesus raised the bar for us when it comes to sexual sin. He says,

> *"You have heard the commandment that says, 'You must not commit adultery.' But I say, anyone who even looks at a woman with lust has already committed adultery with her in his heart."*
>
> MATTHEW 5:27-28

Where our thoughts go is just as important as where our actions go. Did you know you can't think two thoughts at the same time? We have to be diligent in our thought life and choose our thoughts carefully. If impure thoughts are frequently crossing your mind...STOP! RUN! Repent, turn and change! Grab the Word of God and run to safety! I can promise you, Jesus is ready to cleanse, restore and strengthen!

We serve a Holy God; therefore, we are to be holy...pure...blameless before Him. How? By confessing and asking God to forgive our sin in our thoughts and actions. We need regular spiritual baths and for the Holy Spirit to cleanse us. We need repentance. Just like David desired from God in Psalm 51, we need these as well:

- To Be Purified
- To Be Reinstated
- To Restore our Joy
- To Be Free of Guilt
- To Have a Clean Heart
- To Be Loyal Again to God
- To Be Reunited in Fellowship with God

I love the fact God knows what I think, what I feel and where I stumble. So if He already knows, it makes no sense to hide from Him. Why do we do this? The voice of sin can get pretty loud at times shouting, "GUILTY!" "SHAMEFUL!" "UNCLEAN!" The devil does an excellent job trying to keep us from truth, freedom and purity. Why? Because he knows if we truly get a hold of really understanding repentance and turning to God daily with all things, then he loses his grip in our lives. As we repent and turn from sin, allowing God to cleanse and pour His love on us….we become stronger and stronger. We leave the sin behind and move forward with God! We walk in freedom! We experience yet again the joy of our salvation and become a vessel fit to help others. We position ourselves to be a "Nathan" to someone else! Now that's great love!

> *"Restore to me the joy of your salvation, and make me willing to obey you. <u>Then I will teach your ways to rebels, and they will return to you.</u>"*
>
> PSALM 51:12-13

Let's pray out loud,

"Heavenly Father, I repent of any sexual sins, in thought or in action. I don't want any idols in my life to stand between me and You. I turn from these sins and I ask You to cleanse me, my heart and my thoughts. Let my mind think Your thoughts and my ways be pure and holy. Help me RUN to You, to a place of safety knowing You will help me and protect me as I am obedient to you. Lord, I desire to be free! Where I'm weak, make me strong in You! I choose to think on You! I choose to let go of sinful ways and look to You to teach me godly ways.

In Jesus' Name, AMEN."

Now, let me pray for you based on Philippians 4:8-9. Read and receive,

"Lord, by your power, help my brother or sister fix their thoughts on what is true, honorable, right, pure, lovely, and admirable. Empower them to think about things that are excellent and worthy of praise. Strengthen them to keep putting into practice all they have learned, received and heard from Your Word. Let your peace cover, protect and fill their hearts and minds daily. In Jesus' Name, AMEN!"

CHAPTER FIVE

Repentance vs. Worldly Sorrow

In 2 Corinthians 7:8-10, Paul writes:

"I am not sorry that I sent that severe letter to you, though I was sorry at first, for I know it was painful to you for a little while. Now I am glad I sent it, not because it hurt you, but because the pain caused you to repent and change your ways. It was the kind of sorrow God wants his people to have, so you were not harmed by us in any way. For the kind of sorrow God wants us to experience leads us away from sin and results in salvation. There's no regret for that kind of sorrow. But worldly sorrow,

which lacks repentance, results in spiritual death."

2 CORINTHIANS 7:8-10

From the looks of things, Paul played a "Nathan" role like in Chapter 4. Not to just one person, but to a whole congregation! In 1 Corinthians, Paul was pretty heated and very bold at correcting things going on in the church of Corinth. Remember, these were born-again, spirit-filled believers, yet they were living double lives. They were zealous for God and preaching Jesus as the Way, but sexual sin was in the church. They were living carnally and fleshly, and not taking any actions to correct their behavior. So Paul sent the people a letter! He even referred to the letter as "severe." Paul loved the people in the church of Corinth so much and it pained him to convict and correct them, but he knew for their sake, he had to do it. He also knew it was his job as an appointed, chosen man of God.

Joy filled his heart when it was reported back to him that the people responded with repentance and turning back to God. Paul describes a sorrow that can come with repentance and it doesn't harm us. The kind of repentance that makes us run to God and run away from sin! Paul says we shouldn't regret this kind of sorrow. For this kind of sorrowful heart cleanses and purifies and restores us back to God.

Then he mentions another kind of sorrow...worldly sorrow. He clarifies this worldly sorrow is void of repentance and leads to death. If worldly sorrow is lacking repentance, then it lacks God in the equation. Let's look at an example of this with the final days in the life of Judas Iscariot.

Judas was one of the twelve disciples and he was the treasurer for the 3 1/2 year ministry of Jesus. He walked with Jesus, saw the miracles, fellowshipped with him, and believed Jesus was going to become a king. Yet he hoped for a different kind of king. Judas wanted a king who would set up a kingdom where he would be promoted to a major role. When he realized this was not going to work out, he betrayed Jesus. This man did not have a pure heart for people, ministry, or Jesus. Exactly what was the condition of Judas' heart? In Luke 22:3, scripture says,

> *"Then Satan entered into Judas Iscariot, who was one of the twelve disciples, and he went to the leading priests and captains of the Temple guard to discuss the best way to betray Jesus to them."*
>
> LUKE 22:3

In Matthew 26:15, Judas willingly asks the leading priests, *"How much will you pay me to betray Jesus to you?"* He goes to the these priests and accepts money to lead an army to arrest Jesus. Judas' heart and mind didn't just go into betrayal mode overnight. What was the spiritual door Satan entered through to be able to dictate Judas' actions of betrayal? Judas was an offended, resentful and bitter man. To go so far as betraying a friend...a godly friend... there had to have been hatred and anger in his heart brewing for quite a while...more about this in the days to come.

Yet something happens after Jesus is arrested, bound, and condemned to die. Something happens on the inside of Judas and he realizes he has made a huge mistake.

> *"When Judas, who had betrayed him, realized that Jesus had been condemned to die, he was filled with remorse. So he took the thirty pieces of silver back to the leading priests and the elders. 'I have sinned,' he declared, 'for I have betrayed an innocent man.' "*
>
> MATTHEW 27:3-4

Judas was filled with remorse and yes, filled with sorrow. He even acknowledges he sinned and had betrayed Jesus. Judas was trying to desperately fix his heart...to fix his circumstances. The same Satan who filled him to be able to act out betrayal was the same Satan who was now heaping overwhelming guilt and regret upon him. Unfortunately, the priests couldn't cleanse and restore the heart of this man. They tell him at the end of verse 4, **"What do we care? They retorted. That's your problem."** They did not care about Judas feeling better, nor what happened to him. At this point, the money Judas was paid didn't feel like compensation, revenge or reward. He was hopeless and at a place of spiritual death. This led Judas to commit a tragic suicide.

We know from scripture this betrayal of Judas was prophesied, but do you ever wonder what would have happened if Judas had taken his sorrow to Jesus? After all, Jesus loved Judas. In John 13:21, the scripture describes how Jesus felt knowing Judas was about to betray him.

> *Now Jesus was <u>deeply troubled</u>, and he exclaimed, "I tell you the truth; one of you will betray me!"*
>
> JOHN 13:21

Jesus wasn't deeply troubled just because he was about to be betrayed. He knew His whole purpose was the cross. He was emotional because Judas had been with him from the beginning of his ministry. He was his friend. Knowing what Judas was about to do distressed and hurt Jesus deeply.

Worldly sorrow and repentance are not the same. Repentance is taking your sin straight to God, not to man. It is good to apologize when you have hurt someone, but a heart-change and a mind-change can only come through repentance and turning to God. Otherwise, you have not changed and will likely repeat the same sin.

Let's look at another man who betrayed Jesus to the point where he lied and said he didn't even know Him. One of the other twelve disciples, Peter, walked the same path

Judas did on the journey with Jesus. Yet Peter had a different heart. He, James and John spent personal time with Jesus at a level different from the others. Peter knew Jesus was the Messiah. He had a heart sold out to Jesus, but he was still just like me and you…he had a flesh…and he couldn't always see through the eyes of faith. After Jesus had been betrayed and was sentenced to death, Peter had three opportunities to acknowledge he was a friend of Jesus. He denied them all, then proceeds to go into seclusion and weep bitterly for betraying his friend.

Having spent so much intimate time with Jesus, this broken man, Peter, had a heart so different from Judas. Scripture doesn't specifically tell us how Peter repented or how he prayed during his time of deep sorrow, however, we do know that heaven was listening and well aware of Peter's condition.

Go with me to the moment after the death and resurrection of Jesus. It is Sunday morning and an angel is at the tomb to give instructions to the women who were there. After he tells them to "not be afraid" and "He is Risen!" the angel says something which grips my heart every time I read it…

> "Now go and tell his disciples, <u>including Peter</u>, that Jesus is going ahead of you to Galilee. You will see him there, just as he told you before he died."
>
> MARK 16:7

What? The angel makes it a point to say, "Hey ladies, make sure you tell <u>Peter</u>." Those tears Peter shed and the cry of his heart made it up to heaven. Heaven heard Peter's heart. The Lord had forewarned Peter he would betray Him, and he would sin, but He also told him He would be praying for him, because Satan was after him. Jesus knew how Peter really felt about him and Peter was the Rock He would build His future church on!

What an amazing God we serve! Full of grace and mercy! When we are broken, confused, hurting and feel totally lost, our Jesus is there. So many times through fear and deception, we make wrong choices. Jesus knows Satan is after us and wants to "sift us like wheat." Jesus even says,

> *"But I have pleaded in prayer for you, Simon (Peter), that your faith should not fail. So when you have <u>repented and turned to me again</u>, strengthen your brothers."*
>
> LUKE 22:32

Jesus is praying for us! When we repent and turn to Him, He will use us to strengthen others! Nothing wasted! Praise God we have a High Priest who understands. Hebrews 4:14-16 says it best,

> *"So then, since we have a great High Priest who has entered heaven, Jesus the Son of God, let us hold firmly*

> to what we believe. *This High Priest of ours understands our weaknesses, for he faced all of the same testings we do, yet he did not sin. So let us come boldly to the throne of our gracious God. There we will receive his mercy and we will find grace to help us when we need it most."*
>
> HEBREWS 4:14-16

In the Gospel of John, Chapter 21 (read), we read about a beautiful reunion between our risen Lord Jesus and Peter. The last time Peter saw Jesus was at the crucifixion. Peter is now out fishing and Jesus appears on the shore. When Jesus calls out to Peter and he recognizes Him, Peter jumps in the water and swims to shore! I can just see Jesus smiling as He watches Peter swim in record time! In their reunion time together, Jesus asks Peter three times, "Do you love me?" and three times Peter gets to say, "Yes!!!" I love visualizing those three previous denials washing away from Peter's heart and mind with every "yes" he voices to his Lord.

In 1 and 2 Peter, we have the privilege of reading the wisdom from Peter, which comes from his personal mistakes and weaknesses. Jesus was right; Peter did pay it forward to help others. For example, because Peter experienced the deception of the enemy through fear and lack of faith, he boldly tells us,

> *"Stay alert! Watch out for your great enemy,*

> the devil. *He prowls around like a roaring lion, looking for someone to devour. Stand firm against him, and be strong in your faith."*
>
> 1 PETER 5:8-9

This man goes from experiencing times of weakness, fear, doubt, and deception to being filled with the Holy Spirit on the Day of Pentecost (read Acts 2). He goes from denying knowing the Lord, to preaching by the power of the Holy Spirit...so powerfully that in one day he baptized 3,000 people in the name of the Lord! Peter's call on his life was now clear, and all that Jesus had taught him now made sense. Because of the Holy Spirit, he could see, think, talk and understand with a spiritual, eternal perspective, rather than a human perspective. More about the Holy Spirit in the chapters ahead!!!

> *"Come and listen, all you who fear God, and I will tell you what he did for me. For I cried out to him for help, praising him as I spoke. If I had not confessed the sin in my heart, the Lord would not have listened. But God did listen! He paid attention to my prayer. Praise God, who did not ignore my prayer or withdraw his unfailing love from me."*
>
> PSALM 66:16-20

"Heavenly Father, there have been times I have listened to the voice of the enemy and not the voice of the Holy Spirit. There have been times I have denied You when I should have shared my relationship with You. Lord, I repent and ask for Your forgiveness. For the times I have desired more of what I thought the world could offer, rather than desiring You, I ask for Your forgiveness. Lord, fill me with Your Spirit and make me bold like Peter. I turn to You Lord, and I hand over to You my mistakes, guilt, failures and shortcomings. I repent and ask You to cleanse me of any offense, resentments or anger I have left unchecked. Where the enemy has used these against me, I praise You that You can use them to strengthen me, teach me, and as a testimony to help others. Open my heart, my mind and my voice to say, "YES" over and over to You, Jesus! Thank you for how You love me. I love You Lord! AMEN!"

CHAPTER SIX

Repenting For Our Nation

As Christians we are called to unite with purpose, to lift up the name of Jesus and bring glory to God! So if being united as one is important to the spiritual call, wouldn't it make sense that Satan's number one purpose is to divide? Whether it is marriages, families, churches, cultures, ethnic groups, races, etc., the enemy's agenda is to divide, divide, and divide. There is no strength in division because the number goes down.

In school, I loved multiplication. Memorizing all the sets of numbers was fun to me, even though I wasn't great at math. I liked the "x" symbol! What's weird is I never liked division. I didn't even like the symbol...it was confusing, especially when you had a remainder! You never have this issue with multiplication...the number just gets bigger! Having a remainder was so "uneven" to me. Here's an example of division at its worst... dividing up into teams... with a remainder!!! See, you get my point!

More and more we see this great country being divided. Division weakens a nation and when a nation is weak, it loses its freedoms. The United States has turned away from God for years and years and if the Church doesn't step up in prayer, voice, and action, we are in trouble in the days ahead. Throughout history when a nation became prideful and turned from God, disaster was not far away. This country has had Christian roots from its birth and it's time we turn our hearts and minds back to Almighty God. A political party or government cannot turn this ship around...only the prayers and actions of the people of God. God's view on praying for a nation has never changed.

> *"Then <u>if</u> my people who are called by my name will <u>humble</u> themselves and pray and seek my face and <u>turn</u> from their wicked ways, I will hear from heaven and will forgive their sins and restore their land."*
>
> 2 CHRONICLES 7:14

What a wonderful promise from God... "If" we will do our part. Now more than ever we need healing in the United States. It's time to arouse from our slumber. It's up to the Body of Christ to make a difference. As the people of God, we are called to pray, seek (repentance) God, turn and ask for His presence to help.

You may ask, but how does one person get started? Let's see what Moses did in Exodus 32 (read). Moses led God's people, the Israelites, out of Egypt and out of a life of bondage. God led them through the wilderness, yet cared for them in such amazing, supernatural ways. He uniquely provided for them and loved them, yet they continued to grumble and complain. So sad to say, but in our country we are very much like this. God blesses us with so many opportunities, privileges, abundance and choices...more than any other country in the history of time, yet we can act like spoiled brats. We've lost sight of the blessings and the hearts of being a people of gratitude and thanksgiving. Instead, we want more and decide to make unwise decisions apart from God. That's what the Israelites did. They chose to make their own golden calf to bow down to and worship. They did unspeakable and detestable things, forgetting how God delivered them from the brutal slavery of Egypt. This ungrateful behavior in thought, heart and action angered God to the point where he tells Moses (v 9),

> *"I have seen how stubborn and rebellious these people are. Now leave me alone so my fierce anger can blaze against them, and I will destroy them. Then I will make you, Moses, into a great nation."*
>
> EXODUS 32:9

I confess, if I had been Moses, I would have said, "Yes, Thank you God." I would have been so fed up with those people that the possibility of eliminating the belly-aching, paganism, and sinfulness would have been welcomed. But Moses didn't do that….He humbly asked God to forgive them. He stood in the gap, interceded on the people's behalf and asked God to please be merciful. He reminded God how he brought Israel out of Egypt with His mightiness and compassion. Disaster was about to hit the Israelites, but God listened to Moses. Make no mistake, a cleansing had to be done among the people, but Moses praying turned things around.

If we as believers had the heart of Moses, could we turn this country around? After all, we are the delivery system for the Gospel of Jesus Christ. We, as a nation, have always been the leader in taking the Gospel out into the world. When we, as the Body of Christ, are full of the power and love of God, it will not only change this country, but also impact the world. My pastor said one Sunday morning, "Be a part of something larger than YOU!"

Would you be willing to take time to pray for this country and our leadership daily, as well as praying for this world? Just one person praying makes a huge difference, but it requires ALL believers to turn this ship around. We can spend so much time focused on the evil and darkness in the world, yet wouldn't it be better if we become brighter lights? Matthew 5:14-16 gives a beautiful visual of this,

> *"You are the light of the world – like a city on a hilltop that cannot be hidden. No one lights a lamp and then puts it under a basket. Instead, a lamp is placed on a stand, where it gives light to everyone in the house. In the same way, let your good deeds shine out for all to see, so that everyone will praise your heavenly Father."*
>
> MATTHEW 5:14-16

When we turn to God and spend time in His presence and get to know the character of God through the Bible, our light will automatically get brighter. In a broken, lost, and sinful world, there is nothing more powerful than the Church of Jesus Christ. As believers, we have the great honor and privilege to stand before God and repent on behalf of the United States. We are not a perfect people. We are flawed and inconsistent; therefore we need a perfect Savior to help us.

When we spend time with other believers, we become stronger. Surround yourself with people who desire to know

God more fully. Choose to fellowship with people who speak words of faith and sharpen you as a believer. Be the kind of person who speaks encouragement and speaks words of faith to others, instead of words of fear, doubt, complaining and grumbling. Choose to speak words of truth, kindness and love. If you have been in the routine of pointing out the negative and unknowingly "calling forth" the bad that can happen…STOP! Listen… I'm learning this even in my fifties! It's not my opinion, judgment or criticism that's needed. We are called to be the mouthpiece of Christ.

Also, did you know that many times when we are inconvenienced in life, for example with our schedules, deadlines, time, or change of plans…God may be setting up or positioning us to be a blessing to someone? Hold off on the complaining and grumbling just because things aren't going our way. God may be behind the unexpected inconvenience, because He wants to bless us! We don't want to miss a potential blessing!!! Hey, to overcome and resist complaining IS a blessing within itself! Let's use our mouth as an instrument for God, not for the enemy! Whether we are speaking, praying or singing…we are God's instruments!

Imagine one person singing a simple song, like a beautiful solo. Then imagine ten people singing that same song…a group. Then imagine 100 people singing that same song…sounding more like a choir! Then imagine 10,000, then 100,000, then 1,000,000…singing the same song OUT LOUD!

It would be the sweetest sound to our Lord, while deafening to the enemy!

> *"Unseal my lips, O Lord, that my mouth may praise you. You do not desire a sacrifice, or I would offer one. You do not want a burnt offering. The sacrifice you desire is a broken spirit. You will not reject a broken and repentant heart, O God."*
>
> PSALM 51:15-17

God loved us so much that He sent His only Son to be our sacrificial lamb and to shed His blood for us. He tore the Temple curtain that separated us from Him. Through Jesus we can repent of our sins and the sins of this nation. He desires our hearts yielded to Him in repentance. We can choose to dedicate our lives to God's purposes and walk holy before Him as an act of worship. How?

> *"And so, dear brothers and sisters, I plead with you to give your bodies to God because of all he has done for you. Let them be a living and holy sacrifice—the kind he will find acceptable. This is truly the way to worship him."*
>
> ROMANS 12:1

Daily, we can proclaim in worship "He is good! His faithful love endures forever!"

Daily, we can humble ourselves and pray for this country. Daily, we can repent and turn to God.

We are the Church! We are powerful when united as one! Jesus spoke of us in Matthew 16:18, when he told the disciple, Peter,

> *"Now I say to you that you are Peter (which means 'rock'), and upon this rock I will build <u>my church</u>, and all the powers of hell will not conquer it."*
>
> MATTHEW 16:18

The Greek word "rock" means "like a rock, by reason of his firmness and strength of soul." That is our foundation. We are not weak! We are strong in our minds, our wills and our emotions BECAUSE of Jesus. We just have to believe and walk out who Jesus has already said **WE ARE!**

Jesus prayed to the Father,

> *"Just as you sent me into the world, I am sending them into the world. And I give myself as a holy sacrifice for them so they can be made holy by your truth. I am praying not only for these disciples but also for all who will ever believe in me through their message. I pray that they will all be one, just as you and I are one—as you are in me, Father, and I am in you. And may they be in us so that the world will believe you sent me."*
>
> JOHN 17:18-21

Join me in praying…

"Almighty God, we come into Your Temple, not with the sacrifice of animals, but with humble, repented hearts, and through the blood that Jesus shed on the cross. Open up our eyes to Your plan and purposes. Keep our focus on You and let us shine for You, so we can be a bright light for the Kingdom of God. Lord, we stand in the gap and repent for the sins of the United States. Please forgive us for turning our backs to You and hardening our hearts to Your love and provision. Forgive our evil ways and pour out Your Spirit on us once again. We declare that the gates of Hell will not prevail against the Church, because Jesus said so and we choose to enforce it! We choose to stand for Jesus! We are Willing! For His Glory. AMEN"

"Godliness makes a nation great, but sin is a disgrace to any people."

PROVERBS 14:34

SECTION TWO

Would You Be Willing To Receive?

In this section we will look at what it means to be good receivers. You would think being a good giver is better than a receiver, which when it comes to relationships with people, yes, we need to be world class givers. But in order to do this and do it effectively for the Kingdom of God, we need to learn how to be good receivers from God. After all, my giving has little eternal value, unless it is touched by the Lord, and ordained by Him. Apart from Him I can do nothing, but through Him I can do all things! (**Read John 15:5 and Philippians 4:13**)

I find when my giving is not authorized by God, or I do it

to feel good about myself, to impress someone, or out of duty or guilt, then the results tend to go flat, or even backfire. If my motive for giving is out of my own selfish ways, then when the response is not what I expected, I may end up feeling angry, embarrassed or hurt. Have you ever experienced this?

On the contrary, if God has instructed my giving, whether in action, words or my time, then I really don't consume myself with the response or outcome. If my motivation is to please God first, then my motive is pure and blameless! Plus, when I am being obedient to Him, the performance pressure to please others is gone and there's more freedom and joy in the act of giving.

Now let's switch gears and talk about the word "receive" or "receiving." Isn't it interesting the word "receive" can be a positive word to some…as in a gift, money, reward, or a compliment. To others it can be a negative word, especially if they have had a past with abuse, discouragement, betrayal, or harsh words. They can be very skeptical about receiving, because historical experience says, "this may not be a good thing and I have to be cautious."

When we are taught about God for the first time, usually it's presented as you come to God, ask for forgiveness, and then **receive** Jesus as Lord and Savior. What a great plan if you are a good receiver and grew up with people you could trust. But for some, they only decide to participate in half of the deal…they get the repenting down pat, but have no clue how to receive from God. Oh, it's easy to say the words, but the heart and mind can choose to stay guarded. Or maybe choose to accept the salvation gift from Jesus, yet question the Lordship...after all, the mind may think, "how can I trust Him when others have let me down?" If this person is you, I want you to know I am so sorry. I pray that throughout the next six chapters the Lord will bring whatever healing, love and experience you need to help you wholeheartedly **RECEIVE**.

The spiritual truth is this...in order for this amazing, transforming, supernatural relationship with God to flourish...for example, being born again and then afterwards walking in relationship with a loving Heavenly Father and truly making Jesus Lord in our lives; well...we have to accept the whole package. We have to believe and **RECEIVE**. Why? And what exactly are we receiving?

CHAPTER SEVEN

Don't Stay Silent

Words are powerful. They are truly containers of power and authority. Words can heal, encourage and share. Words can also crush, betray, and be destructive. Words can communicate hope or communicate fear. In the Christian walk, words are crucial to our receiving freedom and blessings. Words are also what sets us apart, or at least SHOULD set us apart from the words of the world. The way we use words can be influenced by who we spend time with, because words we hear and take in on a regular basis will eventually come out of our mouth. Jesus said,

> *"A good person produces good things from the treasury of a good heart, and an evil person produces evil things from the treasury of an evil heart. What you say flows from what is in your heart."*
>
> LUKE 6:45

There is a connection between our heart and our mouth. Whatever is in the heart, will eventually come out of the mouth…good or bad. Consider these scriptures:

> *"May the words of my mouth and the meditation of my heart be pleasing to you, O Lord, my rock and my redeemer."*
>
> PSALM 19:14

> *"The heart of the godly thinks carefully before speaking; the mouth of the wicked overflows with evil words."*
>
> PROVERBS 15:28

Based on scripture, we have to get our heart right with God, so good stuff can flow from our mouth. Then we have to actually open our mouth and choose to speak His way. So what does this have to do with receiving?

In Chapters 1 through 6, we talked about the power of

repentance. Going to God and asking for forgiveness, having a change of mind and turning to Him. When it comes to a relationship with God there has to be an EXCHANGE before change effectively occurs. I can repent of sin and come to God, turn to God, but if I don't receive from God...forgiveness, mercy, grace, love, etc., then lasting change will not take place. Transformation will not take place. The desire to want to change and please the Lord will not continuously grow in my heart, therefore, growing daily in a relationship with God is hindered. Why? I haven't received. I'm not fully receiving HIM and what He is offering me. It becomes one-sided.

Think of it this way. I really like appliances, especially the kind which makes housework quick and easy. My favorite is a dishwasher. What a great invention! Let's say I didn't have a dishwasher and I was washing tons of dishes by hand. I become weary of all those dirty dishes and I tend to complain about it. You come to me and say, "Mary Jo, I'm giving you the free gift of a dishwasher!" And I say, "Well, how generous...thank you." You have the dishwasher shipped to my door and there it is in the box. Day after day, I keep it in the box. I don't open it, install it, and therefore I don't use it. You did your part...you gave a great gift, but I didn't do my part of <u>receiving</u> it and putting it to use. Instead, I continue to do dishes like I've done them in the past. I try to wash faster, and buy better cleaning products, but it doesn't help. I fuss and complain, yet I never change my routine. Oh, I remember the gift you gave me and I appreciate your generosity, but I leave it in the box. What a waste of a great gift!

Believe it or not, we can easily do this with God. We ask for forgiveness, but we willingly don't receive. Sometimes it just seems too easy to receive by faith. We think we still have to fix ourselves, or maybe we have just been afraid to say out loud, "God, I choose to receive your forgiveness! God, I open my heart to You and receive all of your good gifts!"

It's time to break the cycle. Time is short and we need to practice being good receivers from God. If you have never been good at opening your mouth and speaking words to receive from God…for ANY reason, it is time to start. It's time to discover you have a voice and it is powerful for the Kingdom of God. And the most powerful words you can speak are HIS WORDS…the WORD OF GOD! For example, let's use the two scriptures mentioned at the beginning of this section and personalize them for the purpose of receiving. Speak these scriptures OUT LOUD, believing and receiving….

"Jesus, I receive and choose You as my Vine. I choose to remain in You and You in me, so I can produce good fruit, because apart from You, I can do nothing." (based on John 15:5)

"Lord, I receive your promise that I CAN do EVERYTHING though Christ, who gives me strength." (based on Philippians 4:13)

Just like a child learning to talk, we have to use our words to speak and proclaim the Word of God. God's Word is powerful and sharper than any double-edge sword (Hebrew 4:12-13). Speaking His Word increases our faith, changes and heals our heart, strengthens our spirit and most of all, helps us get to know our Wonderful God, more and more. He loves us so much!

My younger daughter is great with toddlers and I hear her all the time encouraging "new talkers." She says to them over and over, "Use your words." She pushes them to not use grunts, hand gestures, or pouting, and instead teaches them to express themselves with WORDS!

It all starts with being willing. Start with saying YES! Come on...I'll do it with you!

"Heavenly Father, I confess that I have been afraid, or maybe unclear about the importance of receiving from You. Lord, I want to be a good receiver, because You are a good God, who is full of love and blessings. I ask You to cleanse my heart and mind of harsh, abusive words that were spoken to me in the past. I also ask You to cleanse me from negative and doubtful words I have used out of my own mouth. I want Your words to be my words. I desire to talk like You and for my mouth to be used for Your glory. Help me see You always as a Good Father and give me the courage to let go of fear and doubt and just open my heart

to receive. Let receiving from You become routine, where I can joyfully say to you daily, I choose to receive from You, Father, because I am willing! In Jesus name, AMEN!"

Now, can I pray for YOU? Receive...

"Lord, Thank you for my friend. Thank you for their courage to step out in faith and receive good things from You. I apply the powerful, precious blood of Christ to their mind and ask you to cleanse wrong words from their past. Holy Spirit, pour an oil of anointing over their head right now and let every wrong thinking, ungodly words and fears just slide off in the name of Jesus."

Satan, I command you by the authority of Jesus Christ to release my friend. You were defeated at the Cross and my friend walks in victory because of the Cross.

"Lord, pour in my friend a fresh filling of Your Spirit so they can receive freely, with no fears, doubts, or confusion. Fill them with a joy that looks forward to receiving daily from You! In Jesus Name, AMEN!"

> *"And so I tell you, keep on asking, and you will receive what you ask for. Keep on seeking, and you will find. Keep on knocking, and the door will be opened to you. For everyone who asks, receives. Everyone who seeks, finds. And to everyone who knocks, the door will be opened."*
>
> LUKE 11:9-10 (JESUS SPEAKING)

CHAPTER EIGHT

Receiving Like A Child

Years ago a friend of mine was describing to me a difficult time in her life. She was broken, hurt and discouraged. I felt so sorry for her as she described the pain. Then her countenance changed as she described her healing from God. She said, "The Lord spoke to me and said, 'Come to Me as a child and let me hold you.' So I closed my eyes and pictured myself as a little girl. I crawled up in my Heavenly Father's lap and snuggled in His huge arms. I received His tight hug around me. I let Him wipe the tears from my eyes, and brush the hair back from my face. I remained still and just received all of His love, protection, and assurance that I was His little girl and nothing could ever change this truth."

As she shared, tears rolled down her cheeks and she radiated with joy and peace. As I watched her and listened to her, I thought to myself, "I want that!" It never dawned on me I could come to God as "little me!" This challenged my thinking, my imagination, my faith, and frankly, made my flesh really uncomfortable. But I wanted it! Jesus says,

> "I tell you the truth, anyone who doesn't <u>receive</u> the Kingdom of God <u>like a child</u> will never enter it."
>
> LUKE 18:17

Why a child? Maybe because children are more trusting and life is simpler. They receive easily, instead of justifying, analyzing, intellectualizing, and logicalizing...even though that really isn't a word. When we are little, we are less aware of "self." Somehow in the Lord's presence I am less aware of my hair, clothing, intelligence, or social skills. Seriously, He is God, so there is nothing to hide from the One who knows all about me. He designed and created me, so He knows every hair on my head and I am the apple of His eye. (Luke 12:7, Zechariah 2:8) It is an incredibly transparent place to be... when you are willing to let yourself go there.

So years ago I prayed and asked God to help me be childlike with Him. I asked Him to take me to a place I loved and I invited Him to be there with me. I sat quietly with my

Receiving Like A Child

eyes closed and just waited. In my mind's eye I saw the ocean and I saw me...little. I can't say every detail was clear, but I saw this little girl playing on the beach...and yes, with Jesus. His attention seemed to be on me. He was smiling as I twirled for him in my white, flowy dress. Then I jumped in His arms and laid my head on His shoulder. He held me and I knew I was safe. It was nighttime, yet I wasn't cold. The ocean waves were crashing hard, but I didn't care because I wasn't looking at them. I was facing the other way! I was with Jesus and I was safe, so nothing else mattered.

Since then, when I need to just be quiet and sit with Jesus, or when the "ocean waves" seem to be crashing in my life, I'll close my eyes and go back to the beach. It is real to me. It puts things in perspective for me. I just have to choose to <u>receive</u> Him...again and again.

> *"Then Jesus called for the children and said to the disciples, 'Let the children come to me. <u>Don't stop them</u>! For the Kingdom of God belongs to those who are <u>like these children</u>.'"*
>
> LUKE 18:16

He's calling for the "children"...me and you, no matter how old we are! We just have to come to Him "little." What's stopping you? Pride, trust issues, intellect, shame? Yes, we have to be responsible and be mature, but I am talking about time with Jesus and being free!

Ask yourself…"What is stopping me?" If you feel like some of your childhood was robbed from you, then it's time to take a leap of faith and jump into the arms of Jesus. You need a "do-over" that only Jesus can provide. Are you willing to trust Him? Without receiving and walking with Jesus with childlike faith, you can feel stuck and stale in your Christian walk. Walking in childlike faith also means you may not understand or see all of the "whys" that God is doing, yet know you have a Heavenly Father you can trust.

I'll offer another suggestion. If receiving doesn't come natural, ask God to show you someone who does it well, and then spend time with them. Practice receiving. Over the years I have had to get better at receiving…from God and from people. Receiving made me uncomfortable. Something as simple as a friend wanting to buy me a cup of coffee somehow made me feel guilty or obligated. It took me pressing through the uncomfortable feelings and choosing to receive on purpose.

Would you be willing to be "little?" Would you be willing to start a new practice of receiving God's unexpected gifts and blessings? There are many He wants to give…RECEIVE!

I feel led to pray for you today. After you read the prayer, would you be willing to take a moment in quietness, close your eyes, trust the Lord, and receive?

"Heavenly Father, Would You give my friend a willing heart to be "little" right now? To step out in faith and come before You as a child. To relax in your arms, where it's safe, quiet, and full of acceptance. Lord Jesus, hold my friend and let your abundant love bring peace, comfort and assurance that You are mindful of every detail of their life. By Your Spirit, let them know that You see them, and they can trust You. In your matchless name, AMEN!"

CHAPTER NINE

Let's Start With The Basics: Forgiveness

I know what you are thinking...not another lesson on forgiveness!!! If you have been a believer for longer than a day, you probably know the importance of forgiveness. You have probably heard the preaching over and over... "if you don't forgive others, then God can't forgive you." And yes, this is the truth based on God's Word. Forgiveness sums up the Cross of Jesus Christ. He died and took our place so God could forgive us and restore right relationship with us. Without the Cross, there is no forgiveness of our sins; therefore, it's a fundamental, foundational principle to understand, receive and walk in.

Forgiveness is easy for some, yet hard for others, based on experience. Forgiveness has the power to set us free, but without it, we can stay bound. It is not based on a feeling, but the willingness to choose to forgive and let go. It removes the person, the past, a situation or a circumstance out of our hands and puts it into God's hands. Forgiveness says, "I choose not to try and collect a debt impossible to collect." Forgiveness says, "I choose to let God restore me and make things right because I belong to Him."

Let's take the idea and principle of forgiveness one step further and see what the benefits are to being quick to forgive. Why? Because it truly is a topic of great importance and it can set you free and keep you free!

In Matthew 18:21-35, Jesus tells the parable of the unforgiving debtor. This teaching is prompted by Peter asking Jesus how many times he should forgive his brother who has sinned against him. First of all, Peter is referring to someone he has relationship with…a brother. And Peter even throws out a number…"forgive seven times?" So obviously Peter has forgiven this person at least once or more. I wonder who he is talking about? To forgive more than once means Peter is in close relationship with this brother…probably every single day. We know he has spent the last three years with Jesus and eleven other disciples, so my guess is it has to be one of them. Andrew? After all he was his own flesh and blood. Family can certainly stretch our forgiveness more than anyone else. Could it have been John? He did call himself the "Beloved," which could have gotten on Peter's nerves. I'm going to put my money on John, because in the Gospel of John, he calls himself "the disciple Jesus loved" many times. I can't help but laugh at John when he penned in his gospel,

> *"Peter and the other disciple started out for the tomb. They were both running, but the other disciple outran Peter and reached the tomb first."*
>
> JOHN 20:3

OK, the "other disciple" he's referring to is HIMSELF! He really thought it was necessary for us to know he outran Peter? Well, whoever the "brother" was, it bothered Peter so much and got under his skin daily, he just had to ask, "Hey Jesus…exactly how many times do I have to forgive?"

Peter was serious. He wanted a number! If Jesus would just give him a number, then he would have his permission to say, "I'm done! I've reached the number Jesus said, so I'm finished forgiving you!"

But what Jesus says I'm sure shocks Peter…. "Seventy times seven." In other words, you just keep forgiving and forgiving and forgiving. Because Jesus does this for us…RE-FORGIVING, if you will. Again and again and again….as we REPENT and RECEIVE.

The other part is when you are on the other side and

YOU need forgiveness. When you know you have sinned, gossiped, offended, etc. When you know because of what you said, thought, or acted upon, you HAVE to get right with God…and you want the forgiveness with the person you are in relationship with!

Oh, Praise God! We HAVE to practice the very thing we are asking God to do for us! God has forgiven us a tremendous debt we could have NEVER repaid. We have to be really good at receiving forgiveness, so we become excellent at extending forgiveness to others. I don't know about you, but I need the mercy of God's forgiveness daily.

Let's get practical with this concept and spiritual truth. So many times we focus on big picture things, and we become careless with the little offenses robbing us of freedom and joy. We ignore small situations, which if left unchecked, can build hardness in our heart and can keep us from forgiving others.

Let's look at a simple example. You are in the checkout line at a grocery store and the lady in front of you pulls out a handful of coupons to scan. You are in a hurry, but there is someone behind you, so all you can do is wait. When the lady finally finishes and walks off, the person behind you says, "Can you believe it? They need a checkout line just for those couponers." Without even thinking you agree with the person and say, "I know, I'm in a hurry and so too many coupons are just inconsiderate." As you get in the car, the

Holy Spirit convicts the judgment and harshness in your heart and words:

STOP AND PRAY OUT LOUD, *"Father, I am so sorry I judged the lady and I am sorry for agreeing with the person behind me and letting my words be so unkind. I repent of this behavior. I now turn and receive your forgiveness in Jesus' name. I also ask you to bless the lady and also the lady behind me. Forgive her remarks as well, in Jesus name."*

I know this may sound simple and trite, but left unchecked, it can happen again. In fact, Satan can easily rope us into a situation where he hopes to use our words to gossip, judge, find fault, or have a bad attitude. Over time, without practicing forgiveness and receiving forgiveness, the heart hardens, we ignore the Holy Spirit's nudges, and therefore our witness as a Christ follower is in jeopardy. Listen, Satan knows he can't tempt me to rob a store...but he definitely tries to tempt me to roll my eyes at someone IN the store! Repent! Receive!

Let's go back to Peter. For him to bring this subject up to Jesus means it was an area REALLY bothering him. He was at the end of his rope with this brother. It was on his mind day in and day out. He wanted answers, because he was tired of struggling with it. Do you have a similar relationship? Is it like a weed that keeps popping up over and over? Does it rob your joy or steal your peace? Sometimes it hits close to home in your heart or maybe literally...in your home!

One more scripture to think about,

> *"Love prospers when a fault is forgiven, but dwelling on it separates close friends."*
>
> PROVERBS 17:9

There is a direct relationship between love and forgiveness. This scripture clearly says that our love grows in a positive way when we walk in forgiveness. Which also means holding on to unforgiveness can bankrupt our ability to love. If we think about this logically it makes perfect sense. It's like saying good water and dirty water can equally flow from the same source. As long as there is dirty water, clean water can't exist. We can't afford to settle for an ineffective, spiritual mixture! When we keep our lives clean of unforgiveness, resentments, bitterness, offenses, and keeping records of wrong… then we are a vessel flowing freely to love. And that kind of love looks a lot like Christ's love for us…unconditional, merciful, and abundant!

I'd like to ask you to visualize any person or situation you may be holding unforgiveness towards. You see it? You see them? Now, <u>in your mind turn around</u> and see yourself walking ten paces away from them or the situation. Now drop to your knees and focus on God. Don't turn around… stay there in the scene and receive as you pray this prayer…

"Heaven Father, I ask You to forgive me for holding unforgiveness, offenses and even bad attitudes towards others. I realize that it's doing damage to my heart and weakens my sensitivity to Your voice as well as hinders my love walk with others. Help me to be quick to forgive and quick to receive. Holy Spirit, I ask You to show me areas that I have let unforgiveness grow in me, that are causing my heart to harden. I desire to release people, situations, my past and circumstances, ALL to You. I willingly lay it all at the foot of the cross. In exchange, I choose to RECEIVE Your forgiveness, peace, strength and love. Lord, teach me how to pray and have compassion and love for others, while recognizing situations that trigger me in a negative way. Help me Holy Spirit to discern and be watchful for the enemy and especially when he tries to lead me to sin. I am willing to receive and submit to You...

In Jesus' name. AMEN!"

CHAPTER TEN

You Are God's Favorite!

When I was a new Christian a mentor of mine asked me, "Mary Jo, did you know you are God's favorite?" I really wasn't sure how to process this. Favorite? Me? Favorite is such a strong word. It means chosen over someone or something else. When she asked me this, I wasn't sure if I should be proud, honored or really, really scared. And exactly what was it about me that made me God's favorite? She then burst my bubble by saying, "And I am God's favorite too!" Wait, can you have two favorites?

Actually when we accept Jesus as Lord, there is a "favor" placed on us...a mark. We belong to Him...ransomed from death and brought into the family of Almighty God. This powerful God wanted me...and you...to be in His family. He couldn't stand the thought of living without you, so He became your substitution and died for you so you could live with Him. Sometimes it's hard to wrap our minds around this, because we see our flaws, as well as our weaknesses and our sins. In Psalm 8:3-4, David writes,

> *"When I look at the night sky and see the work of your fingers—the moon and the stars you set in place—what are mere mortals that you should think about them, human beings that you should care for them?'*
>
> PSALM 8:3-4

I confess, I think about this scripture a lot. When I am praying and I am really down on myself, I think, "God, look at me...why do you care? In the big picture, why do I matter to you?" Do you ever do that?

One time I was driving through the Rocky Mountains in Colorado on the way to a campsite. I had been marathon driving for over 18 hours and was "running on fumes" and so very tired. Through a stretch of a few miles, the mountains were on both sides looking as tall as skyscrapers and the curve of the road was extreme. The road was narrow and the mountains were huge and majestic. I gripped the steering wheel so tight my knuckles were white. It was so hard to keep my eyes on the road because the view was overwhelming. It seemed like at any moment they could easily swallow me up! I had a sudden realization of being very, very, very, small. It was a revelation that in comparison to God, I was tiny…yet He was aware of me.

Have you ever read the Book of Esther? (read) It's a great story in the Bible and if you have never read it, now's a good time! I want to hit the high points of this story and how we are like Esther.

Esther was a young Jewish girl who, among many Jews, had been exiled from Jerusalem to Babylon as slaves. During this time there was a king who reigned over 127 provinces. His queen embarrassed him one night in front of his wealthy guests and politicians at a party, so his advisors convinced him to banish her, and choose another queen. He agreed and within just days, thousands of virgins from all over these provinces were brought to the kingdom for this "beauty contest." Esther was among the many, and each young girl went through a year's worth of pampering before she could even come before the king. Remember…Esther did not ask for this opportunity, nor did she volunteer. Esther was chosen.

All of the girls' "pageant coaches" if you will, prepared them for their one and only shot at impressing the king. Through the wisdom of Esther's coach, it was decided her natural beauty would do the talking. No bling, no glitter, no bright colors, no false eyelashes….just herself. So with no sales pitch or marketing strategy…Esther meets the king. And the king chooses Esther. She becomes the chosen queen.

Out of thousands of young, beautiful girls, do you think Esther looked at them and said, "Wow, I can't compete with them? They are more beautiful, talented, taller, smarter…." Do you think Esther thought over those 365 days of preparation, "Why would I be chosen?"

As the story continues, we discover there's a plot to have the Jewish people destroyed. Why? The king's right-hand man, Haman, is evil and totally despises Esther's uncle, Mordecai. Mordecai works at the palace and by the king's request, all palace officials should bow before Haman when he passed by. Mordecai refuses to bow or show Haman respect.

Haman hates Mordecai so much he not only wants to kill him, but all of the Jews too. So he talks the king into issuing a decree to destroy them in all the provinces, telling the king the lie that the Jews are a rebellious people to the kingdom. Little does Haman know…Esther is Jewish. She has hidden her ethnicity.

Mordecai tells Esther about the plan and encourages her to talk to the king. But Esther knows to walk into the king's throne room unannounced was instant death. Mordecai believes Esther did not become the queen just by chance. He knew she was chosen. And he knew she had <u>favor</u>.

Mordecai may have had confidence in Esther's position, but Esther wasn't so sure. She was so terrified that she asked all the Jews in the palace to pray and fast. Esther knew she was just a normal girl. She had no idea why she was chosen and why the king favored her over others...but he did. Oh, we can read the story and see how God chose Esther for the job and supernaturally had the king favor her, but what if you were Esther? She knew her weaknesses and flaws. Even though she now wore a crown on her head, she also knew the rules of the palace.

As Esther courageously enters the throne room unannounced, the king smiles...and extends his scepter to her...welcoming her to share and ask whatever she wants. Long story short, Haman is destroyed and the Jews are safe. Why? Favor.

You may think you are nothing special, or you are "small" like being in the midst of mountains. But the truth is, YOU ARE CHOSEN. God actually chose you before you chose Him. Yes, you had to accept Him and RECEIVE Him as King. Nevertheless, He chose you! Therefore, He favors you! You are a favorite! As though you wear a crown on your head! He extends His scepter of goodness and mercy to you daily. He smiles when you enter His presence.

What assignment has He prompted you to do? What nudges have you had? What are the desires of your heart? RECEIVE His Favor! You are a child of the King. Listen to what Peter writes about believers,

> *"For you are a chosen people. You are royal priests, a holy nation—God's very own possession. As a result, you can show others the goodness of God, for he called you out of the darkness into his wonderful light. Once you had no identity as a people; now you are God's people. Once you received no mercy; now you have received God's mercy."*
>
> 1 PETER 2:9-10

We are to be walking, talking vessels of God's goodness in the earth. Not because we are eloquent, skilled or trained, but because when we receive from Him, we have favor. Choose to believe you are favored by God…especially when you don't "feel" like it!

One of my favorite scriptures is Acts 4:13. Peter and John, now filled with the Holy Spirit, stand before the religious priests, rulers and teachers of the religious laws to explain and defend how a man was healed by the power of the name of Jesus. They speak boldly, and point blank share that salvation ONLY comes through Jesus Christ. The response of these religious experts always encourages me.

> *"The members of the council were amazed when they saw the boldness of Peter and John, for they could see that they were ordinary men with no special training in the Scriptures. They also recognized*

them as men who had been with Jesus."

ACTS 4:13

The "ordinary" can do the "extraordinary" when we are filled with the Holy Spirit and spend time with Jesus! I want to be recognized as someone who has been with Jesus! I want my life to reflect Him! I'll gladly be His favorite. Will you be His favorite with me? Then RECEIVE!

"Almighty God, Just like Esther, I choose to believe and receive that "I AM CHOSEN." Lord, even though I may not see the plan, or know the details, I trust that it is a good plan...a God plan. Because I spend time in the Word and fellowship with Jesus, I receive that others will recognize that I belong to You and I will be an effective witness for the Kingdom. Lord, I give you my dreams and desires and I trust You to show me when and how to pursue them. I receive the patience of timing, the gift of boldness, and the joy of belonging to You! Jesus, my heart's desire is for You to be my priority daily. And out of our relationship, I can be a better "me" because I'm more like "You." I praise You Lord that I am blessed and highly favored by You! In Jesus' name, AMEN!"

CHAPTER ELEVEN

Someone's Following You!

Nobody likes being followed unless it's for good. Have you ever watched a drama where the main character is being followed. They realize they are being followed and think the person trailing them has the intention to harm them. Then at some point in the movie it's revealed the person was there for protection...for doing good.

As we journey through this life we all face many challenges, disappointments, sorrows, places of confusion and pain. You may be going down one of these paths now. You are trying your best to follow Jesus, but there are times He seems miles away. You're trying to stick close to Him, especially when unexpected trials happen, but life can take a toll.

If you've read the Gospels, you see over and over how people followed Jesus. Verse after verse says things like,

> *"And they left their nets at once and followed him."*
>
> MATTHEW 4:20

> *"They immediately followed him…"*
>
> MATTHEW 4:22

> *"Large crowds followed him and he healed their sick…"*
>
> MATTHEW 19:2

> *"So he left that area, and many people followed him."*
>
> MATTHEW 12:15

> *"The crowds found out where he was going, and they followed him."*
>
> LUKE 9:11

As we get to know Jesus through the Word of God and build a relationship with Him, we want to do what people did in the Gospels...we want to follow Him! Just like them, we don't always understand His ways, His timing, or what He may do next, but we want to follow. When we pray, we are following Him. When we fellowship with other believers, we are following Him. When we serve and minister to others, we are following Him. When we read our Bible, we are following Him.

There are two scriptures in the bible that are NOT my favorites. Here's the first one:

> *"I have told you all this so that you may have peace in me. Here on earth you will have many trials and sorrows. But take heart, because I have overcome the world."*
>
> JOHN 16:33

Jesus told the disciples this. I like the "take heart" and He has overcome the world! I just don't like the "you will have many trials and sorrows." I wish he would have said it this way, "I have overcome every trial and sorrow so you never have to experience one on earth, so take heart and enjoy your peace!"

Here's the other one:

> *"Dear brothers and sisters, when troubles come your*

> *way, consider it an opportunity for great joy."*
>
> JAMES 1:2

Seriously, we are only at verse 2, and James starts in on us having troubles! He then goes on to say it's a good thing, because it will test our faith as well as grow our endurance, and other character building stuff. James is a short book in the New Testament, but boy can he give an attitude adjustment and encourage the believer to grow up!

As much as these scriptures are hard to take, they are very true. We all go through trials while following Jesus, which is no doubt far better than going through a trial NOT following Jesus. What's been your trial?

- Death of a loved one
- Lose of a job
- Divorce
- Cancer
- Betrayal
- Taking care of an elderly parent
- A wayward child

Mr. Trials and Mr. Sorrow seem to be the bad guys coming after us like in the movie and it feels like we are running for our lives! We do all of the things we know to do, yet we sometimes feel Jesus is in the distance and we can't seem to stick close to following Him. My question then is, "WHO IS FOLLOWING YOU?

At the end of Psalm 23, there is a beautiful promise which has brought me so much comfort and peace over the years when I have faced a trial. Most of the time you hear this Psalm at a funeral, or maybe it was one you memorized in Sunday School. Let's look at the last verse in the King James Version,

> "Surely <u>goodness and mercy</u> shall <u>follow me all the days of my life</u>: and I will dwell in the house of the LORD forever."
>
> <u>PSALM 23:6</u>

You are being followed! God's Goodness and God's Mercy are following you!!! As you follow Him, never doubt He is following you! He hasn't left you. He is close. Trust in this powerful promise.

Let's go a little deeper with this amazing verse, to really digest what God is saying. My prayer is you'll have a visual that will fix in your mind to strengthen you as you walk through trials and sorrow. Sometimes we lose the richness of the meanings of words through the English language. I was blessed with an incredible spiritual mentor, who taught me and gave me a love for the Hebrew and Greek translations… and even a love for the Webster Dictionary! Let's dive into some Hebrew in this verse!

Goodness—good things, pleasant, agreeable to the senses, excellent, rich, valuable in estimation, prosperous, happiness, bounty

Mercy—goodness, kindness, faithfulness and unfailing love

Shall Follow—to be behind, follow after, pursue, run after, chase, harass, aim to secure

Of My Life—living or alive; as in green like vegetation, flowing like fresh water, or like springtime

Now let's put this together to really see what God is saying…as if we were watching on the "big screen!" To me, these descriptions fill my spiritual ears and eyes with God saying something like this,

"My goodness and mercy are like a bounty of rich, valuable treasures full of my loving kindness. I want you to have them so much that I desire to pursue and chase you down so close that one would think I was harassing you. I am so close behind you that you should feel secure and protected. I want your life to be like the new growth of springtime, or like a fountain of fresh flowing water."

Oh My Gosh!!! Can you see it? God isn't hiding behind bushes, peering out hoping we don't suspect He's following us. No, His Goodness and Mercy are chasing us down! His unfailing love and kindness are breathing down our neck!

For years during flip-flop weather, my daughters and I would be in a store and either one or both would be following behind me so close, that they would step on the back of my shoes! I would usually trip, or my shoe would fall off! That's how close Goodness and Mercy are! They WANT to trip you up for the good! Yet if we aren't aware then we don't know it's available to RECEIVE!!!!

Because He is such a loving God, there are times when I need a little reassurance He's following me. So I'll pray for myself or for someone else in a tough place:

"Lord, I need to see a glimpse of your goodness in this situation."

"Lord, I need your mercy to overtake me today."

"Lord, let my friend experience your unfailing love in her circumstance."

God knows I am flesh and blood, and I know He is my Heavenly Daddy. I have never once felt His disapproval when I ask to experience His goodness, mercy and love. Sometimes I'm reminded He is close when a friend calls to pray with me, or He will have someone text a scripture. Or sometimes He will send me a redbird, or an amazing sunset! He knows exactly what will speak to me and what will remind me that He is mindful and He is close by. And He knows what you need too! You can trust Him following you. RECEIVE!

Now that you have a visual of God's Goodness and Mercy, it's time for you to take the initiative and pray to

God. No prayer below. You go to Him…Talk to Him… and RECEIVE…all the days of your life!

CHAPTER TWELVE

VIP

Have you ever met someone you thought was really important? Maybe a celebrity or someone you had much respect or admiration for? One person for me is a Christian singer named, Carman. In the early 90's, when my daughters were little, I would play Carman videos for them. (If you don't know who he is you can YouTube him!) This amazing Christian man presented the gospel in such unique, theatrical ways which ministered to all ages. From the time they could walk, my daughters loved dancing and singing with him via television. One day I was eating lunch with my best friend in Nashville, TN. My younger daughter was with me and was only 2-years-old at the time. I looked over and there was Carman eating with friends. I was not going to miss this opportunity, so I grabbed my baby girl and made my way toward him. As he looked up, I politely said, "I'm sorry to disturb you, but I just wanted to tell you how much your music and ministry has meant to my family, especially my daughters." Carman extended his hand and said, "Well, thank you so much", as he shook my hand like the perfect gentleman. Then he turned to my two-year-old, extends his arms and says, "Well hello, can I have a hug?" My daughter, with star-struck eyes, throws her little hands out and walks right into his arms for a big hug. She knew exactly who he was! So precious, except for the fact that I got a handshake and she got a hug!

The reason I thought Carman was important and what drew me to his ministry was his gift and boldness to enforce the power of God, to preach, teach, minister and help set people free. And I recognized that Carman knew the MOST important person to know…because He is the most important person I know….the Holy Spirit.

In John 16:5-15, Jesus describes the person of the Holy Spirit to the disciples:

> *"But now I am going away to the one who sent me, and not one of you is asking where I am going. Instead, you grieve because of what I've told you. But in fact,*

> *it is best for you that I go away, because if I don't, the <u>Advocate</u> won't come. If I do go away, then I will send him to you. And when he comes, he will convict the world of its sin, and of God's righteousness, and of the coming judgment. The world's sin is that it refuses to believe in me. Righteousness is available because I go to the Father, and you will see me no more. Judgment will come because the ruler of this world has already been judged. There is so much more I want to tell you, but you can't bear it now. When the <u>Spirit of Truth</u> comes, <u>he will guide you into all truth</u>. He will not speak on his own but will tell you what he has heard. He will tell you about the future. He will bring me glory by telling you whatever he receives from me. All that belongs to the Father is mine; this is why I said, 'The Spirit will tell you whatever he receives from me.'"*
>
> JOHN 16:5-15

Jesus breaks the "bad news, good news" to the disciples. He has to leave, because if He doesn't the Holy Spirit cannot come and do His job. This person is the third person of the Trinity. Three in One...Father, Son and Holy Spirit. One God – Three distinct roles. For example, I am Mary Jo, yet I am a mother, daughter and sister. One person, yet three roles.

Another example is a lamp...you have the body or structure of the lamp, the light bulb and the cord to plug in for electricity. You have to have the structure (God), and you have to have the light bulb (Jesus/The Light)...but without the power of electricity (The Holy Spirit) the lamp isn't complete. Without the person of the Holy Spirit, we are without a power source that Jesus intended for us to have.

When I was growing up, the only thing I knew about the Holy Spirit was He was at the end of the prayer... "In the name of the Father, the Son and the Holy Spirit. Amen." Or he was referred to as the Holy Ghost, which made him, in my mind, kind of mystical or too spiritual to get to know. When in fact, He...not an "it"...He is the person Jesus WANTS me to have a relationship with. Jesus was trying to explain to the disciples that even though they wouldn't understand Him leaving their presence, it was the best deal because then He could be with them ALL of the time...living IN them... THROUGH the Holy Spirit. He even tells them that if they would just listen to the Spirit of Truth, He would guide them into ALL truth.

Let's get really practical. Imagine you are hired as a teacher. You are trained, know the material, have a love for teaching and students, and are so excited to guide them on their academic journey. On your first day of school, they tell you that you can't go into the classroom! There is a room full of students, yet you are not allowed to teach and guide them. You watch them struggle to make choices, to learn and be in relationship with other students, yet you are not allowed to help. You know you can make a huge difference in the way they live, learn and how they could have a better future, yet you have to sit and watch while over and over they flounder. You are not appreciated or welcomed.

Now let's picture another kind of scenario. You are hired to teach and the school welcomes you with open arms. The students realize quickly how much they can learn from you, and ARE WILLING to let you teach and help them. You guide them in wisdom, choices and comfort them when they've had a bad day. They can depend on you to be there for them and they look to you to help with all situations, questions and concerns...whether big or small. You have so much love for them, and they know you'll always speak truth to them. What a wonderful feeling to know that you are appreciated and depended on to perform your job daily.

On a very small scale, this is the job of the Holy Spirit. The Holy Spirit is our Teacher, Counselor, Helper, Comforter, Standby, Advocate, Intercessor, Strengthener, and Guide. When I go to the Word of God, I need a teacher. As I invite Him daily, He always points me to Jesus and He opens up things in the Word that I would never grasp in my own understanding. When I'm sad, He comforts me. When I'm confused, He helps brings clarity. He's underestimated, and underappreciated, yet Jesus said <u>listen to Him</u> and be <u>filled with Him</u>! Let's look at Jesus' instructions to the disciples after He was resurrected.

Forty days after the crucifixion, Jesus appears to His followers more than once to convince them He was alive. As He was eating with them, He tells them,

> *"And now I will send the Holy Spirit, just as my Father promised. But stay here in the city until the Holy Spirit comes and fills you with power from heaven."*
>
> LUKE 24:49

> *"Do not leave Jerusalem until the Father sends you the gift he promised, as I told you before. John baptized with water, but in just a few days you will be baptized with the Holy Spirit...."But you will <u>receive</u> power when the Holy Spirit comes upon you. And you will be my witnesses, telling people about me everywhere..."*
>
> ACTS 1:4-5, 8

I love the way Jesus describes the Holy Spirit as "a gift." What is consistent about gifts from God is we can't earn them, match them, create them or deserve them. This is true with His gift of salvation (Romans 6:23, Ephesians 2:8-9), spiritual gifts (1 Corinthians 12:4-11) His gift of grace and forgiveness (Romans 5:15-17) and the gift of peace (John 14:27). The only thing we can do with a GOD GIFT is RECEIVE it!!!

I doubt the followers really understood the utmost

importance of receiving the Holy Spirit the day Jesus told them. Jesus could have told them many things before he was lifted up to heaven, yet telling them to wait and **receive the power of the Holy Spirit** was what He shared. If the Holy Spirit is important to Jesus, then He should be important to us. This also tells us, by receiving the Holy Spirit, we are equipped to share and witness about Jesus. Scripture says there is a power of sin working against and through us. I don't know about you, but I need a greater power not only to free me from the power of sin and death, but a power to help me beyond what I can do in my own strength. Jesus broke the power of sin at the cross, but I have to **receive** and walk it out!

One of my favorite prayers from the Apostle Paul is in Ephesians 1:16-23. I'd like to pray this prayer for YOU! Would you be willing to RECEIVE? The Holy Spirit is the greatest VIP in the earth...there is no better friend you can have... RECEIVE,

> *"I have not stopped thanking God for you. I pray for you constantly, asking God, the glorious Father of our Lord Jesus Christ, to give you spiritual wisdom and insight so that you might grow in your knowledge of God. I pray that your hearts will be flooded with light so that you can understand the confident hope he has given to those he called —his holy people who are his rich and glorious*

> *inheritance. I also pray that you will understand the incredible greatness of <u>God's power for us who believe him</u>. This is the <u>same mighty power that raised Christ from the dead</u> and seated him in the place of honor at God's right hand in the heavenly realms. Now he is far above any ruler or authority or power or leader or anything else—not only in this world but also in the world to come. God has put all things under the authority of Christ and has made him head over all things for the benefit of the church. And the church is his body; it is made full and complete by Christ, who fills all things everywhere with himself."*
>
> EPHESIANS 1:16-23

The person of the Holy Spirit is someone I could talk on and on about. Today I would like to challenge you to learn more about Him and how to more fully cooperate with Him. This is an ongoing relationship. Remember, this is the most important relationship you'll ever have on this earth. We need the Holy Spirit now more than ever before. Would you be willing to pray and receive? Receiving the Holy Spirit will change your life! Receive this precious, priceless gift!!!

"Lord Jesus, Thank You for sending the Holy Spirit to live in me and through me. I believe and receive Him as Your precious gift to me.

Holy Spirit, I welcome You into my life. No matter my

level of understanding about You, I am willing to learn more, yield more and receive more. I need You, Holy Spirit. I need You to empower me daily. I need You to teach me the Word, counsel me, and bring me truth on a daily basis. Holy Spirit, be my helper and remind me to invite You daily into my life....as the best and most important friend I'll ever have. Teach me how to be Your friend and to trust You in all I say and do. I rely on You to convict and correct me daily and I desire to cooperate more fully with You. In Jesus' Name, AMEN!"

> *"I pray that God, the source of hope, will fill you completely with joy and peace because you trust in him. Then you will overflow with confident hope through the power of the Holy Spirit."*
>
> ROMANS 15:13

SECTION THREE

Would You Be Willing To Reclaim?

Welcome to the third section...RECLAIMING! I pray you have been practicing the beauty of repenting and receiving from God. It's something I have to be intentional with when talking to God and asking the Holy Spirit to continue to teach, guide and counsel. It takes effort, humbling ourselves, and wanting to see God bigger in our lives. John the Baptist said,

> *"He must become greater and greater,*
> *and I must become less and less."*
>
> JOHN 3:30

In order for this to be an ongoing reality, we have to get really good at transactions with Jesus…a continuous giving and receiving. A daily "laying down" my ways and "picking up" His ways. Friends, it has to be practiced because our fleshly, soulish nature is wired to say, "But I want, but I think, but I feel." We can be such selfish creatures, therefore being selfless, serving and keeping our focus on Jesus has to be practiced often.

We also must read and study the Bible to get to know the character of God and what His opinion is on how to live in this world as a Christian. The ways of the world, culture, trends and popularity seem exciting, yet are often deceptive. What we hear, see, and feel can seem like God, and even sound quite spiritual, but does it line up with scripture? I'm always sobered by how Jesus handled the religious people of His day. They were so religious in the way they talked and by keeping the spiritual law, yet their hearts were far from God. Jesus told the Pharisees,

> *"Outwardly you look like righteous people, but inwardly your hearts are filled with hypocrisy and lawlessness."*
>
> MATTHEW 23:28

Ouch!!! They weren't interested in truth or change of heart…they wanted prestige, fame and recognition. They wanted a form of religion and godliness, yet apart from truth, transformation and yielding to God. So yes, this world can pull on our hearts and minds, but the question has to be, "What does God say?"

My goodness it is a battle, but Praise God, He helps us! As the Body of Christ, we are called to strengthen and encourage one another. I'm standing with you on this journey! Some days it may not look like it or feel like, but by faith we are transforming...from glory to glory! It's an inside-out job!

Now, let's talk about RECLAIMING. I really like this word because it is such an action word. It's a visual of going into the enemy camp and taking back what was stolen or rightfully ours! It is not going in timid, but with force, confidence and an "I will not be defeated" attitude. This powerful word is the synonym to words like: reacquire, recapture, recover, recollect, recoup, regain, repossess, retake and retrieve. Not to mention, replenish, redeem, repurchase and rescue. Whew! That's a lot of R's!

Why is reclaiming so important? Because we all have places in our lives that were either stolen from us, or we willingly gave away. I'm not talking about material things, but places in our thoughts, emotions, and our choices. Without even understanding the spiritual ramifications, we made choices that jeopardized our heart, our mind, our body, or our emotions.

With repenting and receiving from the Lord, we make amazing spiritual transactions with God that cleanse and begin making us whole again. But there can be places in our lives that we have to reclaim. Here's how you can identify spiritual places that need to be RECLAIMED. Most have an "I am" statement we hear in our heads, because it's a lie we still believe defines us. For example,

- I am shameful because of impure choices I made before marriage
- I am unwanted because my parents divorced
- I am powerless because of a childhood experience
- I am unlovable because I was overlooked by a loved one
- I am a failure because I should have made better choices
- I am stupid because I made bad grades
- I am guilty because certain situations in my past feel like my fault

Logically, we can know truth, yet still in our emotions we will go to what we have experienced in the past, rather than what we know is the truth in the present. It can feel like all the repenting and receiving can't get rid of the torment of past mistakes or experiences. Powerful, negative words spoken over us still seem to echo in our minds, no matter what our age.

Repenting and receiving sets us free from the sin issues,

but what about the regret issues? What about places in us that need to be healed and made whole? Sometimes there can be confusion in our thinking. Satan would like for us to believe that if we don't FEEL different, or if the memories still torment our mind, then maybe God hasn't forgiven us! These lies continue to attack the mind and feel just as true in the present as they did in the past. We can routinely confess scriptures, be positive, and even rebuke the enemy, yet not be experiencing total freedom and victory. Then the question stands, can we ever get rid of the mental accusations, the scenes that continue to replay in the mind, and the lies that won't go away, because frankly, they still "feel" true...even decades down the road?

I have GREAT news! If you are a believer in the Lord Jesus Christ, then you have the right to RECLAIM with His authority! Because Jesus died on the Cross and because He victoriously was raised from the dead, YOU can go and take back from the enemy. As Christians we have been given His authority to TAKE BACK from the enemy! Jesus didn't die on the cross for us to limp along in life and still be burdened down with our past. Jesus is the Light of the World, so if there are dark areas in our life, let's turn on the light! It's a scientific fact that once there is light in darkness, then darkness can NEVER overtake the light. It is most definitely true spiritually. Jesus said,

> *"If you are filled with light, with no dark corners, then your whole life will be radiant as though a floodlight were filling you with light."*
>
> LUKE 11:36

Are you willing to flip the light on? Are you ready to RECLAIM? Let's GO!

CHAPTER THIRTEEN

You Have The Right To Reclaim

A few years ago I had to take care of my dad, because my mom had an accident. While she recovered, I lived with my disabled dad and basically stepped into her role as his caregiver. Taking daily care of him was challenging, but I also had to handle all of their finances. I was a little panicked thinking about paying their bills and dealing with long-term healthcare legalities. Then my mother told me a beautiful thing, "Honey, years ago I had you sign a signature card on our bank accounts and a Power of Attorney form with our lawyer." I had totally forgotten this. She had the foresight to prepare and have legal forms signed just in case I had to step in. I quickly went from panic to peace, because I realized I had legal rights and therefore exercised them.

Can you imagine me going to her bank and saying, "I need to sign my mother's checks, because she's my mother and I love her." They would have said, "We know you love her, but you have no authority over her account." Circumstances change when I say, "I'm on the signature card."

Just like with my mother and father, we can love God and serve Him, yet there are times we need to know, understand and enforce our rights as His children, because He gave us those rights. Jesus dying on the cross for the forgiveness of sins, so that we can have eternal life, is the greatest miracle that will ever happen. Yet the cross, His death, and that precious blood shed just for me and you, gave us so much more than the promise of salvation. That sinless blood and His powerful resurrection gave us legal rights, an inheritance, and a spiritual covenant with promises from God. We were given the authority to "take back" and enforce through the power of that precious blood, with a boldness and confidence.

The word "salvation" doesn't just mean eternal life. In the Hebrew and in the Greek, this amazing word means so much more…**Wholeness, Deliverance, Prosperity, Healing, Protection, Victory, Strength, and Welfare.** So let me ask you this…out of all these words in bold print, which ones will you need in heaven? None of them! Salvation is just as much for my life here on earth as it is for eternity. And Jesus Christ embodied these powerful promises of salvation. He is our _____ ... just fill in the blank with those amazing words in bold! He is the provider of each one! In Psalm 18:1-3 David understands the power of the Lord,

> "I love you, Lord; you are my <u>strength</u>. The Lord is my <u>rock</u>, my <u>fortress</u>, and my <u>savior</u>; my God is my rock, in whom I find <u>protection</u>. He is my <u>shield</u>, the <u>power</u> that saves me, and my place of <u>safety</u>. I called on the Lord, who is worthy of praise, and <u>he saved me</u> from my enemies."
>
> PSALM 18:1-3

Did you know that we are in a battle...a spiritual battle? Whether we like it or not, as believers in the Lord Jesus Christ, we entered into a war. As soldiers in the Lord's army we are called to stand, enforce and declare the promises of God through the Word, the name of Jesus and the blood He shed...and take back or RECLAIM. In the Old Testament, King David understood going into battle with the Lord's authority! Let's look at Psalm 118:10-12,

> "Though hostile nations surrounded me, <u>I destroyed them all with the authority of the Lord</u>. Yes, they surrounded and attacked me, but <u>I destroyed them all with the authority of the Lord</u>. They swarmed around me like bees; they blazed against me like a crackling fire. But <u>I</u>

destroyed them all with the authority of the Lord."

PSALM 118:10-12

Wow! King David credited his victories with the spiritual backing of the Lord's authority! And his victories weren't just by the "skin of his teeth"...the enemies were destroyed!!! That's powerful!! We need that same understanding and faith in our battles!

Make no mistake, the battle was won against Satan when Jesus died on the cross and was raised from the dead. But we still live in a world run by the enemy's system. There is evil in the world...have you noticed? There are accusations, pressures, doubts, fears and temptations that come against us daily, especially in our minds and hearts...have you noticed that too? So how do we reclaim and enforce?

First, we have to recognize (and remind ourselves often) that our battle is not with people, but a spiritual battle. True, the enemy works through people, but we have to stand and believe what the Word of God says about who the enemy is. When the Apostle Paul closes his letter to believers in the book of Ephesians, Chapter 6:10-12 he tells us our position and defines the enemy:

> *"A final word: Be strong in the Lord and in his mighty power. Put on all of God's armor so that you will be able to <u>stand firm</u> against all strategies of the devil. For*

> we are not fighting against flesh and blood enemies, but against evil rulers and authorities of the unseen world, against mighty powers in the dark world, and against evil spirits in the heavenly places."
>
> EPHESIANS 6:10-12

Wow, that's some heavy advice, but very crucial for the believer. We are battling an unseen force, but we can see and feel the effects in our lives, in our minds and against our emotions. Paul tells us we do have the proper equipment to walk out this battle and it will help us to "be strong."

It's not easy being strong. When we face the attacks of the enemy, it's easy to feel the opposite of strong. We feel weak, powerless and totally defeated. Being strong can feel so difficult and sometimes feel like we are just plain terrible at it. For me, it can feel this way because sometimes I miss the point of the rest of Paul's sentence…"Be strong **in the Lord and in His mighty power**." Now that's a game changer! I don't know about you but being strong in Mary Jo just makes me exhausted. I'll easily get worn out, fed up, and feel defeated pretty quick if I'm trying to be strong in myself. But I'm to be strong IN THE LORD AND HIS MIGHTY POWER! Now that tips the scale every time! The battle then moves into the "battle already won" category. There is nothing more powerful than God power!

Next, Paul says we have equipment for this spiritual

battle. If I said visualize yourself as a football player, you would see yourself with a helmet and shoulder pads. If I said visualize yourself as a surgeon in an operating room, you would see yourself with a scalpel, gloves, scrubs and mask. If I said visualize yourself as a police officer, you would see yourself wearing a uniform, badge, and gun. All three of these examples are easy to see and visualize. As a believer, we should just as easily see ourselves in proper spiritual equipment. Our equipment is called spiritual armor and we put it on by faith, because we are like soldiers in a spiritual battle. Let's continue in Ephesians 6:13-17 and see what those armor pieces are,

> *"Therefore, <u>put on</u> every piece of God's armor so you will be able to resist the enemy in the time of evil. Then after the battle you will still be <u>standing firm</u>. <u>Stand your ground</u>, putting on the <u>belt of truth</u> and the <u>body armor of God's righteousness</u>. For shoes, put on the peace that comes from the Good News so that you will be fully prepared. In addition to all of these, hold up the <u>shield of faith</u> to stop the fiery arrows of the devil. <u>Put on salvation as your helmet</u>, and take the <u>sword of the Spirit</u>, which is the word of God."*
>
> EPHESIANS 6:13-17

Paul tells us that yes, there will be times of evil, and this spiritual armor is necessary and we have to PUT IT ON! In your mind, go back to the three examples I gave and visualize yourself again. This time visualize:

- Football player…..see yourself on the field, but your equipment is lying on the bench.
- Surgeon….you are operating on a person, but your equipment is lying on a side table.
- Police officer….you are enforcing the law, but your equipment is hanging in a locker.

Now picture a soldier in civilian clothes standing on a battlefield. Get the picture? Let us, by faith, put on our armor! Now see yourself wearing your spiritual equipment:

- **The Belt of Truth** – Knowing the Truth of God's Word
- **Body Armor (Breastplate) of Righteousness** – Protecting our mind, heart and emotions
- **Shoes of the Gospel of Peace** – Peace with God through the Good News
- **Shield of Faith** – Faith in God protecting us from the enemy's accusations and temptations
- **Helmet of Salvation** – Protection of the mind and assurance of salvation
- **Sword of the Spirit** – The Word of God

What is interesting is each piece of armor is worn by the soldier, except for two...the shield and the sword. We hold our Shield of Faith with one hand to protect ourselves and quench those fiery arrows of temptation that the enemy sends against us. With the other hand we wield the Sword of the Spirit to attack with. We will discuss the Sword of the Spirit in Chapter 15. I encourage you to study the Armor of God. There are books, websites and many teachings that are worth the read! Revelation of this powerful and necessary equipment will make you want to suit up by faith daily!!!

The last thing I want to point out is between Ephesians 6:10-17. There is a word repeated three times...STAND. You would think with the armor on and in a battle, there would be a lot of movement. Like a soldier in a war, there is running, shooting, combat, etc. But in this spiritual armor we STAND. Why? Earlier we said the spiritual battle has been won through the Cross of Jesus Christ. Spiritual fighting is not like earthly fighting. In the Greek, the word "stand" means "to make firm, establish, escape in safety, uphold the authority, steadfast."

The visual is standing still, calm, firm and totally immoveable and hidden in the armor of Christ. Now isn't that interesting that we can RECLAIM not by grabbing, yelling, or getting all heated up, but with a calm confidence in the battle already won. Now that's some powerful armor.

Let's pray,

"Lord Jesus, As my commander and chief in this spiritual war, I choose to follow You. Forgive me Lord when I have focused too much on people and circumstances rather than seeing it as a spiritual battle. I am tired of fighting people. My mind is tired of the discouragement, accusations and temptations. Jesus, I acknowledge that on that Cross, You defeated Satan and stripped Him of power. Through Your death and resurrection, I believe I have eternal life as well as healing, prosperity, protection and deliverance while I live on this earth. Remind me, Holy Spirit, to daily put on my armor by faith, and stand on the promises of the Word. Jesus, Your work on the Cross was complete, therefore I choose to STAND. My confidence is not in myself, but in a Mighty God. Thank You Lord, that the battle has been won. I have the victory in Jesus' Name. Amen"

CHAPTER FOURTEEN

How Do You See It?

In Chapter 13, we took a look at Ephesians 6:10-17. I'd like to discuss a specific verse to bring a better understanding to how the enemy attacks a believer. Let's look back at Ephesians 6:11:

> "Put on all of God's armor so that you will be able to stand firm **against <u>all strategies</u> of the devil.**"
>
> EPHESIANS 6:11

Satan is referred to in scripture as the father of lies. Jesus said in portions of John 8:44,

> "...He has always hated the truth, because there is no truth in him. When he lies, it is consistent with his character; for he is a liar and the father of lies."
>
> JOHN 8:44

Satan works strategies against us, because he has no truth in him. The Greek word used in this passage for "strategies" means, "wiles, cunning arts, deceit, craft, or trickery." He is the master of deception, because he is incapable of truth. When he presents something, like fear, he makes it seem bigger, stronger and more powerful than Almighty God. That is pure, deceitful strategy.

In 2 Corinthians 2:11, Paul writes to the Church of Corinth about the importance of forgiveness for the believer's benefit "*....so that Satan will not outsmart us. For we are familiar with his evil schemes.*" The Greek word used in this passage means, "a mental perception or an evil purpose." When it comes to Satan, he is after the believer's mind and our perception, or perspective.

One of the greatest things we need as a believer is perspective. I want to share a story about perspective. When my older daughter, Ellen, was babysitting for a family years ago, she experienced a major fear attack of the enemy. After she had put the kids to bed she started flipping channels and unintentionally landed on a horror movie. Mesmerized, she stopped clicking the remote and watched just long enough to see and feel terror. She turned the television off, but fear had gripped her mind and the enemy began telling her how bad she was for watching and of course, the scene kept running over and over in her mind. By the time she came home, she was a mess. I began praying over her and telling the fear to leave in Jesus' name, but nothing changed. She was in tears, panicking and feeling defeated with guilt.

Finally, I said, "Holy Spirit, what does she need?" Immediately, I heard the word, "Perspective." I asked Ellen, "WOULD YOU BE WILLING to let the Lord show you something?" She agreed. Totally trusting the Lord at this point I said, "Jesus, would you show Ellen how big this fear is in comparison to You?"

That was all I said and I just waited. After all, I had no strength in my abilities to enforce truth and defeat the enemy's lies, but I did have HIS mighty power and I had faith that my God would do something. As Ellen sat with her eyes closed, I watched her and witnessed an amazing thing. Her countenance changed before my eyes. She went from hysterically crying to total peace. Then a big smile came across her face.

At this point I'm intrigued, so I have to ask, "What happened?"

She almost laughs as she said, "he's not quite as tall as the sole of His sandal."

"What? You mean the fear is the size of Jesus' sandal?"

Ellen corrects me and says, "No, he's NOT quite as tall as the SOLE of Jesus' sandals." We both busted out laughing and she went right to sleep…peaceful and with revelation about the mighty power of God.

Perspective…it's more than a point of view. Did you know the word perspective actually means, "*the art of drawing solid objects on a two-dimensional surface so <u>as to give the right impression of their height, width, depth, and position in relation to each other when viewed from a particular point</u>*." You may have just thought, "WHAT?" Read it again! Wow, our commander and chief, Jesus, wants us to know and spiritually see the enemy's size AND position in comparison to Him. In other words…there is NO COMPARISON!

One of my favorite stories of perspective in the Old Testament is David and Goliath. This story has been told so many times as a children's story, we can easily forget the spiritual principles of this event (To read the story in full, go to 1 Samuel 17).

David is a teenager who Samuel, the prophet, has just anointed as the future king of Israel. God begins positioning David by sending him to King Saul for music ministry and servanthood. A battle is about to take place between the Philistines and Israel. The Philistines keep things simple by sending their top warrior, Goliath, to taunt and challenge the

Israelite army. This 9-foot giant basically shouts, "Send your best warrior to fight me! Whoever loses, that nation becomes the servants!"

The Israelite soldiers shook with pure fear. Just typing this, I'm looking at my 8-foot ceiling in my office. A 9-foot man with the most impressive armor made to fit him would make anyone turn white as a ghost. The Israelite soldiers were looking at Goliath with natural eyes and listening to his threats with their natural ears.

One day as young David was taking lunch to his brothers, who were in the army, he overhears the commotion about this giant's challenge. David asks if there's a reward for killing this man and questions why this man is even allowed to speak and defy the Living God. Already David has a different perspective than these seasoned soldiers. In David's mind, he's thinking, "let me get this straight…you are more afraid of this man than of God?"

David's brothers and the other soldiers laugh at David, but David keeps his spiritual focus. He goes to King Saul and volunteers to fight Goliath. What is his motive? David had a relationship with God and He knew the power of a man was no match to the power of God. David knew when he defended his family's flock of sheep against lions and bears; he wasn't using his own strength, but the power of God. In unwavering confidence David declares,

> *"The Lord who rescued me from the claws of the lion and the bear will rescue me from this Philistine!"*
>
> 1 SAMUEL 17:37

In David's mind and heart, this battle was a done deal before it ever started. David didn't ponder, justify, overthink, or weigh pros and cons in this matter. He opens his mouth and shouts,

> *"You come to me with sword, spear, and javelin, but I come to you in the name of the Lord of Heaven's Armies, the God of the armies of Israel, whom you have defied."*
>
> 1 SAMUEL 17:45

David becomes pretty graphic and tells Goliath how he will kill him, plus he firmly declares for ALL to hear,

> *"This is the Lord's battle, and he will give you to us!"*
>
> 1 SAMUEL 17:47

You probably already know how this ends. With a smooth stone and sling shot, Goliath falls to his death. Goliath's "height, width, depth and position" was nothing in relation to David's perspective of God. He had a spiritual point of view. NOTHING was bigger than David's God. We need this kind of perspective in the days ahead. RECLAIM your focus! RECLAIM your perspective! Stop being so impressed with the giants! Instead, speak like David and say, "I am not impressed!"

Ask Jesus what His truth is when you feel fear, discouragement, defeat, or when your mind and heart seem overwhelmed and you feel powerless. Are you willing to ask and let Jesus show you Truth? It can be the difference in seeing a problem or fear as big as Goliath or seeing it from a "sole of a sandal" perspective. After all, the enemy already knows how he compares to Jesus. In James 2:19, there's a window to how demons feel,

"You say you have faith, for you believe that there is one God. Good for you! Even the demons believe this and they tremble in terror."

JAMES 2:19

So if they know who Almighty God is, shouldn't we? If they shriek in terror at the mention of the name of Jesus, why do we fear? Is anything more powerful than our God?

"But as for me, I will sing about your power. Each morning I will sing with joy about your unfailing love. For you have been my refuge, a place of safety when I am in distress. O my Strength, to you I sing praises, for you, O God, are my refuge, the God who shows me unfailing love.

PSALM 59:16-17

"How great is our Lord! His power is absolute! His understanding is beyond comprehension!"

PSALM 147:5

"Almighty God! There is nobody like You! I ask You to forgive me for focusing on the giants in my life and in my mind. I am weary with feeling overwhelmed and underequipped. Lord, I need a refilling of perspective of who You are, so I can RECLAIM and speak with confidence, "My God is great! He is my Strength! All things pale and are small in comparison to my Conquering King!" I receive Your Truth, Lord Jesus, and I choose to walk in that Truth with my eyes on You! I receive a fresh filling of your power by Your Spirit. Help me be quick to turn my thoughts to You, and daily choose to see from a spiritual perspective. Praise the Name of the Lord! AMEN!"

CHAPTER FIFTEEN

The Sword Of The Spirit

"For the word of God is alive and powerful. It is sharper than the sharpest two-edged sword, cutting between soul and spirit, between joint and marrow. It exposes our innermost thoughts and desires."

HEBREWS 4:12

In Chapter 13 we talked about the mighty Armor of God. Each piece of armor represented a spiritual piece for us to wear as a believer. Just like the armor an Israelite soldier wore, our spiritual armor protects us from the enemy from head to toe. Each is to be worn, except for two...the shield and the sword. To understand more about RECLAIMING, let's study more about the Sword of the Spirit.

What is the purpose of a sword? A sword is for cutting or piercing and for thrusting. In Hebrews 4:12, the Word of God is described to be alive and as powerful as the sharpest of swords. First, we have to understand that the Bible is not just a book. It is the living, breathing, transforming Word of God. For the Believer, it should be our most important, vital, priceless possession.

Sometimes we take for granted the preciousness of the contents of this book. We have many translations to choose from and can purchase one at any bookstore, and in some cases even a grocery store! We can choose the color, size, style and even large print! We have the freedom to carry our Bible with us and sit at a coffee shop and read it.

But what if that leather-bound book was a sword? I'm not talking about a pocket knife, but an actual two-edged sword. Can you imagine trying to walk in any store, shop, church, or airport with a big ole sword in your hand? You are now carrying an aggressive weapon! You would be arrested within minutes!

Yet in so many countries, if you tried carrying this book in hand, we call the Bible, you would be arrested in minutes! Satan knows this book is a sword. He knows it will transform a life as well as render him powerless. No other book in the

The Sword Of The Spirit 161

world is prohibited in certain countries, except for the Bible. Why? Because it is spiritual, not just a "good read."

Why a double-edged sword? First of all, let's look at another scripture which has a powerful visual of this double-edged sword. In the book of the Revelation, the disciple John is exiled to the island of Patmos to live out his last days. John is visited by Jesus, yet He looks very different from the Jesus he walked with for 3 ½ years. What John sees is so unlike anything he's ever seen before, that he does the best he can to describe it. Notice all of the "likes" as we read:

> "When I turned to see who was speaking to me, I saw seven gold lampstands. And standing in the middle of the lampstands was someone <u>like</u> the Son of Man. He was wearing a long robe with a gold sash across his chest. His head and his hair were white <u>like</u> wool, as white as snow. And his eyes were <u>like</u> flames of fire. His feet were <u>like</u> polished bronze refined in a furnace, and his voice thundered <u>like</u> mighty ocean waves. He held seven stars in his right hand, and <u>a sharp two-edged sword came from his mouth</u>. And his face was <u>like</u> the sun in all its brilliance."
>
> REVELATION 1:12-16

As John is doing his best to give a visual of what he sees, he shares a lot of "this looked like this." Until he tells us what is coming out of Jesus' mouth. He doesn't see just any kind of sword, but specifically sees a double-edged sword. That's a wild thing to picture in our minds, but if we combine this visual with Hebrews 4:12 and Ephesians 6:17, the picture gets clearer.

I believe it would make sense to say, if Jesus had a double-edged sword coming out of His mouth, then we should have one coming out of ours! The "Word of God" is not just pages to read. It is "rhema"...a beautiful Greek word that means "uttered by a living voice", "a matter of command", "a spoken message." That sword coming out of Jesus' mouth is powerful! It is the Living Word and we have the Bible to prove it! What makes this Word twice as sharp? God has already spoken it in His Word...now WE have to speak it! First God speaks...spoken once, then we speak it... twice spoken. DOUBLE-EDGED!

Have you ever had a scripture suddenly come to mind? Or maybe you heard your pastor preach and one particular scripture he shared was a "that was for me!" moment? The Holy Spirit didn't just give you that scripture to ponder and think about...He's prompting you to SPEAK it! Yes, out of your mouth. And that makes it a double-edged sword! Just God speaking it through His Word is just one-edged. The believer speaking that Word makes it double power!

Satan is not afraid of the Bible getting in the hands of people. People all over this country have one. What he is afraid of is a person SPEAKING the words of the Bible. If he can keep countries from getting Bibles, then they can't speak it. Yet in the United States, Satan knows Bibles are everywhere, so he has to deceive. If he can keep the believer in a place of complacency, self-absorbed, prideful, worldly, or living by their feelings, then he can shut down the power of the spoken Word. And if he can shut it down, then there's no transformation, no healing, no deliverance, no prosperity, no encouragement, no witnessing, no life....sounds like death to me.

Back to Hebrews 4:12, we see this sword cuts pretty deep...on whom? First, the Word is used on us. To RECLAIM, we have to go to the Word of God, saying, "Lord, change me!" Oh, we pray, beg and ask for God's help day in and day out, but without speaking His word there is no change. You gotta have "rhema!" Here are some examples of letting the Word "cut deep" for transformation and RECLAIMING:

- "Lord, I choose not to copy the behavior and customs of this world, but I will let You transform me into a new person by changing the way I think. Then I will learn to know Your will for me, which is good and pleasing and perfect." (based on Romans 2:12)
- "Jesus, I choose to run from sexual sin! No other sin affects my body like this, because sexual immorality is a sin against my own body. My body is the temple of the Holy Spirit, who lives in me and was given to

me by God. I do not belong to myself, because God bought me with a high price. I choose to honor God with my body." (based on 1 Corinthians 6:18-20; great for reclaiming purity)
- Lord, I choose to get rid of all bitterness, rage, anger, harsh words, and slander, as well as all types of evil behavior. Instead, I choose to be kind to others, tenderhearted, and forgiving, just as You have forgiven me." (based on Ephesians 4:31-32)
- "Since I am chosen by God to be a holy person, whom He loves, I will clothe myself with tenderhearted mercy, kindness, humility, gentleness, and patience. I will make allowance for other's faults and forgive anyone who offends me. Because You forgave me, I will forgive others. I will clothe myself with love, which binds me with other believers. I will let peace that comes from Christ rule in my heart, because I am called to peace. And I will always be thankful." (based on Colossians 3:12-15)

Listen, if you pray this way out loud, transformation will come, your thinking will change and your actions will look more like Jesus. We have to use the Word of God on ourselves to expose wrong thoughts, desires and motives. Only the Word of God helps us understand who we are and who we should be. What we think matters! Our attitudes matter! If you are willing to RECLAIM God's way, you can be free! As I let the Word work on me, then I look more like Jesus every day to the enemy. He's afraid when the Word of God rolls off of my tongue!

We've got our armor to PUT ON. We've got the Sword of the Spirit, which is the Word of God to SPEAK. We have the promises of God's Word to STAND. Let's pray and RECLAIM!

"Lord Jesus, I choose to pick up the Sword of the Spirit. Your Word is so powerful that it can transform me in the way I think, speak and act. I am tired of feeling defeated. I choose to stop believing the enemy and what he says about me. I choose to let go of wrong thinking, wrong words and wrong actions. I choose to let the Word of God define me. I choose to speak Your Word, Lord. I choose not to use this spiritual sword timidly, but I raise it high as I speak Your Word over my life.

Holy Spirit, I trust You to teach me how to wield this sword. As I read the Word of God, teach me how to speak the scriptures over myself, my family, my job, my circumstances, my country and my future. Let the Word perform a major work in me so I can be more like You!

I choose to RECLAIM all my doubts and fears that come against my mind. I choose to RECLAIM the lies that say past mistakes define my future. I choose to RECLAIM peace, instead of believing anxious feelings and fears. I choose to RECLAIM wholeness, joy and hope in my life. I choose to STAND.

In the matchless name of Jesus, AMEN!"

CHAPTER SIXTEEN

Get Off My Land!

Land was very important in the Old Testament. War after war was fought against enemies to claim rights to territory. Still today in the Middle East, most of their conflict and battles are over territory. The huge countries that surround the tiny country of Israel are constantly threatening her because they want this land. Look at a globe or map sometime if you are not familiar with the Middle East and look at the size of Israel. Then look at the size of countries like Iraq, Iran, Saudi Arabia or Turkey. Just like tribes and nations constantly attacked Israel for her land thousands of years ago, today's surrounding countries are still hostile to her because they believe that peace cannot come to the Middle East until Israel gives up her land. This kind of thinking is not even logical, but it IS spiritual. God gave the land of Israel to the Jewish people, forever...period. Yet the enemies of the God of Abraham, Isaac, and Jacob still pursue God's territory and want to take over the land.

As God's children, let's look at this principle from a totally spiritual point of view relating to our own lives. When we accept Jesus as Lord and Savior, He resides in us through the person of the Holy Spirit. When we invite the Holy Spirit to fill us with his presence to teach, guide, and comfort and lead us into all Truth, then it's like asking him to take over our spiritual territory. Our new spirit now belongs to Jesus and through the Holy Spirit we are giving Him permission to be in charge of the land of our soul. But many times this territory has been influenced and controlled by the enemy because of our past. Because of our past choices and experiences, we may still have ungodly influences in our "soulish" territory. This is not a salvation issue, but it is an issue that can still affect our thinking, emotions and our will.

Let's go back to Genesis when God spoke to Moses about leading the Israelites out of Egypt and into a land reserved for His people. Genesis 3:7-9,

> *"Then the Lord told him, 'I have certainly seen the oppression of my people in Egypt. I have heard their*

> *cries of distress because of their harsh slave drivers. Yes, I am aware of their suffering. So I have come down to rescue them from the power of the Egyptians and lead them out of Egypt into their own fertile and spacious land. It is a land flowing with milk and honey—the land where the Canaanites, Hittites, Amorites, Perizzites, Hivites, and Jebusites now live. Look! The cry of the people of Israel has reached me. And I have seen how harshly the Egyptians abuse them."*
>
> GENESIS 3:7-9

God makes it clear this is to be their land...a luscious, vibrant, fruitful territory. He also says that it is currently occupied by enemy tribes. So God is taking His people from a land of bondage and abuse, into a land of godless tribes of enemies. In order to occupy this land, they have to "reclaim" it.

You might ask, "Wouldn't it just be CLAIM the land, since they have never lived there?" No...the land was already CLAIMED by God for His people, but now they would have to RECLAIM and take what God said was theirs. They would now have to drive out these "ites" of people and take this land, which God says, "it's YOURS!" Because God said it was theirs, they can say with confidence, force and authority given to them by God, **"Get Off Our Land!"**

When you met Jesus, a beautiful miracle happened.

Your spirit was born again and you were plucked out of the enemy's hands. Your spirit went from the "bondage and death of Egypt" to the "land flowing with milk and honey." Just like the Israelites, God saw your "oppression" and He heard your "cries of distress and suffering." Salvation was yours to have, but you had to receive it. Your spirit became brand new, but your way of thinking and your emotions still may belong in part to permission you gave the enemy.

Let's get very specific. For example, if you grew up with ungodly thoughts and words from your parents, a sibling, a teacher or especially yourself, then there is spiritual territory in your soul that you will have to take back. I'm not talking about an occasional, "I hate my hair" moment. I'm speaking of year after year after year of saying in your heart and even with your lips things like, "I hate myself." It's like a snowball rolling down a hill getting bigger and bigger. The bigger it gets the more room it takes up.

Then you meet Jesus and you are born again. You know He loves you, but the way you feel about yourself hasn't seemed to go away. Why? Because the devil can rightfully say, "I have permission on part of this territory…because he/she <u>hates</u>." It's been a place of wrong thinking for so long. If "love never fails" then hating is the polar opposite. When a person hates themselves, they are warring against the very image of God. We are created in His image and created by Him; therefore hating ourselves becomes a powerful spiritual force against the believer. The devil doesn't play fair, nor does he leave without a battle. He understands territory and land and he understands permission and legal rights. Therefore, we have to understand our rights to kick him off the land of our soul and RECLAIM it for the glory of God. This word RECLAIM is like using the word RENOUNCE.

Renounce means "to refuse to recognize or abide by, any longer in an agreement or claim." You see, we make agreement with the devil when we harbor for long periods of time emotional sins of hate, anger, resentment, shame, guilt and pride. Just like the Israelites had to go in and RECLAIM the promise land territory from the enemy, we have to do the same. They had spiritual legal rights to take the land...and by having Jesus as Lord of our life...so do we!

So many people go through life understanding repentance and receiving forgiveness from God, but they don't understand why they are not experiencing total freedom from the lies from their past and the emotions that go with them. Let's look at what Jesus said,

> "When the Spirit of Truth comes, he
> will guide you into all Truth."
>
> JOHN 16:13

The Holy Spirit guides or leads us into ALL Truth. His job is to present the WHOLE TRUTH to us...so that we can become WHOLE. He's the most wonderful counselor, who knows our whole timeline, so wouldn't it make sense to trust Him to bring Truth? If He is the Spirit of Truth, then He knows where the "lies" are in us. At the beginning of Section 3, "Would You Be Willing To Reclaim?" I mentioned examples of "I am" statements. Go back to that introduction and look over that list…do any of those statements sound familiar or perhaps apply to you? Or can you think of more accurate "I am" statements that go through your mind frequently and still bother you?

When the Holy Spirit leads, he leads both going forward and also going backwards. If His job is to bring us Truth, then we may have to go back in our mind and heart to where there may be lie statements. Think of "lie statements" as dark corners or dark rooms in our mind where light needs to be flipped on!

Let's use an example from the list and I'll put myself in the scenario. I want to give you a practical example how cooperating with the Holy Spirit has worked in my life. For example, **"I am stupid, because I made bad grades"** could be from a past experience I had in a certain grade level growing up. Maybe a teacher pointed out to the class that I didn't do well on a test and it embarrassed me, therefore, I didn't feel as smart as the others. What would that lie look like? Let's break down the example:

Past Experience: My third grade teacher embarrassed me

in front of the class by sharing my bad test score. It made me feel stupid.

<u>Present Lie</u>: I am stupid. I am not as smart as others.

So the experience of a third grade teacher announcing the grade and embarrassing me would unfortunately be a fact. It happened and therefore, would be a part of my past. But that is not the problem. It is the lie that continues to play in my head…"I am stupid!" Although it's been many, many years later, if I make a mistake in the present, my first thought could be "I am stupid."

Now some of you are thinking, "I wish she wouldn't use the word 'stupid.'" OK, let's get real…lies in your head are NEVER politically correct! They are never polite or soft in terminology! They are LIES, therefore from the enemy, who is never mild or fair. Just a side note.

That lie has to be reclaimed with my authority in Jesus, so I can properly realign myself with what God says about me! He says I have the mind of Christ (1 Corinthians 2:16), but I cannot properly apply the truth of His Word until that lie is kicked out! Kicked off the land of my soul!

Jesus is so personal and He heals and brings truth in so many different ways. He can do that because He is Jesus! Never try to box-in Jesus with a formula or principle. Let Him be Lord, and then choose to cooperate. I am choosing to simply share my personal experience and what has worked for me.

In the above example, what I would do is invite the Holy Spirit to take me to that time period in my mind, and then really lean into how it felt. I would willingly let the Holy Spirit be "The Counselor" and guide the process. It's not always comfortable, but it is that place in my past where the root of the lie began. I would also really feel the "I am stupid" statement while visualizing being in that classroom. I would invite Jesus into the scene and ask Him for His truth. Then I would patiently wait, listen, watch and trust Jesus. Again, this experience and healing can look different for each person. The point is being WILLING to let the Holy Spirit lead. Also, it is not HOW Jesus will heal and bring truth, but rather believing Jesus WILL bring truth because He is merciful, loving and incredibly good!

Asking Jesus to reveal truth to those lie statements is like flipping on a light switch in that dark corner. When you are willing to receive truth from Jesus, then everything changes. Again, if I go back to the example, the teacher embarrassing me by announcing my low test score, well, that would be a factual truth! It would have really happened and yes, I would have really felt like I wasn't smart. But to still feel that way would be emotionally wounding as an adult. I'm continuing to believe a spiritual lie, instead of believing spiritual truth.

We all have places where lies have set up. Places we may have been mistreated, wounded, felt guilty, abused, embarrassed, shameful, etc., and frankly, those experiences are part of the tapestry of who we are. And yes, it is very unfortunate those things happened. Yet when we get older, year after year, it's not what happened that keeps us from more freedom through Christ, but instead, still BELIEVING the lie statements and letting them define us in the present.

Also, I'd like to mention an area that can halt our healing and reclaiming process...anger. If you are holding anger, you need to give it to Jesus. Willingly give it to Him. God's righteousness cannot grow when anger resides in us. Giving anger to Jesus by no means minimizes the experience that produced that anger. Yet I've realized when I carry anger, it affects my body, my soul, and my spirit. It's toxic.

Anger gets way too hard to carry over time. We tend to filter life through that anger, which clouds proper perspective and decisions we make. When you exchange the anger for God's peace, it's like letting Him be in charge of the land of your soul. Ask Jesus to show you what a "territory of anger" looks like compared to a "landscape of peace and freedom." Sometimes it helps to close your eyes and visually see yourself giving that anger to Jesus. Watch Him take it, then ask Him for something in return to replace that anger. Jesus gives good gifts when we are willing to receive them.

Again, you may be thinking, "Mary Jo, this all is sounding a little too spiritual." Well, I should hope so! Look at it this way...in order to expel a supernatural, spiritual lie; we have to have supernatural, spiritual truth. We can't fight a spiritual battle in the natural. Just won't work. Believe me I've tried. It's very tiring, and you'll feel defeated every time. So we learn to use spiritual weapons instead. Remember, you have authority in the Name of Jesus to RECLAIM. You have the BLOOD of Jesus to legally prove it! You have a mighty SWORD of the SPIRIT, which is the Word of God!

When we read about the way Jesus healed, delivered, and brought truth to people, it was always supernatural and amazing. It was always personal and sometimes, SUDDENLY! It was always tough to explain in the natural, but nevertheless lives changed, healings happened, and God was glorified! There's nobody like Jesus!!!

Now it's time to go in prayer, by faith in the power of the cross, and TAKE BACK your territory! If you still feel like your soul territory is dark, fruitless and overrunning with "ites", it's time to clean up the land!!!!

NOTE: Do not rush this prayer time. Take time to welcome the Holy Spirit and just get quiet for a while. Pause when you need to and just focus on Jesus. My prayer is this will not just be a prayer of words, but you will experience Jesus and feel refreshed and renewed!

"Heavenly Father, I come to You in the name of Jesus and I ask You to help me RECLAIM areas of my life that still hold my thoughts and emotions captive. First, I repent

and ask You to forgive me for hating myself in the past and I ask You to forgive me for holding anger in my heart. I don't want to war against myself any longer and I am tired of carrying this anger. I hand over the hate and the anger to You in the name of Jesus. I release it to You. Thank You for taking it. I hand over to You any shame, guilt, resentment, fears, or places where I have had pride. I willingly choose NOT to carry this any longer. In exchange, I receive Your TRUTH. I receive your love, peace, blessings, faith and a sound mind. I receive in Jesus' name."

Now we will address the enemy with the authority Jesus gave us...repeat after me...OUT LOUD!

"Satan, you are a liar and a thief. Jesus is my Lord and the Holy Spirit is my Truth, therefore I renounce the spirit of hate, as well as all of the lies you have held over me. I have nothing in common with you, therefore I command you in the name of Jesus, to GET OFF MY TERRITORY! You do not have my permission anymore. You have to go because I belong to God. I cover the land of my heart and mind with the blood of Jesus. My heart belongs to God. My mind belongs to God and my emotions belong to God. He is my Healer and my Peace. I RECLAIM myself...body, soul and spirit for the Glory of God."

Now we will praise and thank Jesus,

"Jesus, Thank You for your faithfulness. I ask You to fill the land of my soul with the fruit of the Spirit. I choose to receive Your love, joy, peace, patience, goodness, kindness, humility, faithfulness and self-control. Where areas were barren, dark, dry, and full of lies, I receive a fresh filling of Your Spirit. Wash over my heart with Your Living Water. Let the landscape of my life be abundantly fruitful. Help me continuously cooperate with the Holy Spirit and be open to His counsel and revealing more lies in my past. I choose to receive the joy of my salvation and the joy of my future. I choose to believe I am whole in You! In Your Holy Name, AMEN"

Can I pray for you?

"Lord, I am in agreement with my brother or sister in Christ. Holy Spirit, continue to teach, guide, and counsel any areas that need RECLAIMING. Help us to not let the enemy take any part of our mind, will or emotions. Help us daily to welcome the Holy Spirit and give Him permission to point out any area in our lives we need to take back. Reveal and make us aware of every lie we believe to be truth! Expose every lie Holy Spirit and let us RECLAIM with the authority of Jesus! Thank You Lord…You are faithful and You are good. AMEN."

CHAPTER SEVENTEEN

Do It!... (You) / Do / It

When I was in middle-school, one of my favorite things to do in English class was diagramming sentences. Subjects, verbs, adverbs, adjectives, prepositions...they all had a place on the diagram. One day the teacher threw us a curve by introducing Imperative Sentences. An imperative sentence gives a command. It can end with a period, but it can also end with an exclamation point. Because an imperative sentence doesn't have a visual subject word, it implies the subject is "YOU."

This kind of sentence asks or tells people to do something. The word "imperative" actually means, "of vital importance, or crucial." It's not simply "asking or sharing" to give a person an option. Imperative is very authoritative and requires immediate action. It also "implies" that you have the ability to do what is commanded; otherwise the sentence would end with a question mark. For example, I have titled this chapter "Do It!" This means I'm not only expecting you (and me) to "do it," but I know you have the ability to "do it." If I had titled it "Would you do it?", then I am giving you the option to say "yes" or "no."

Why the grammar lesson? The Apostle Paul was the king of imperative sentences. From the book of Romans through Titus, he uses imperative sentences over and over, which means he is commanding us to do them, expects us to do them, and knows we CAN do them.

In this section, "Would You Be Willing To Reclaim?" we have discussed ways to "take back" from the enemy and how to better understand the devil's strategies. We have read about our spiritual armor, and how we don't fight against people, but spiritual principalities. We have read how spiritual forces are real, powerful and we should be aware and knowledgeable. But would you like to know what is more powerful? Our Flesh!

We have a sinful nature, called the flesh. It's that nature we were born with because of the fall of humanity in the Garden of Eden. I don't believe any teaching or scripture proof is necessary to convince you that we are wired to be sinful and selfish. My soul (the mind, the will and the emotions) has to be told and made daily to yield and submit to God's way of doing things, rather than my own.

In Romans 7 and 8 (read), Paul shares his own battle with his flesh, and tells us that this crazy flesh will always be opposed to the Spirit...God's way. Daily, actually moment by moment, we get to choose to live by our feelings and selfish ways or we can tell our soul to "sit down" and we make it obedient to God. We can be our worst enemy in following God. For me, my pride in wanting to be right can get in the way of simply trusting God to handle conflict. Oh, I could blame it on the devil, but sometimes we give him too much credit for things we have the power to change. After all, we are born again believers, filled with the Holy Spirit!!! We have the will to tell our emotions and feelings to hush and lead them in a God direction, instead of a "me" direction.

This chapter is simple. I am going to supply you with many scriptures of imperative sentences to help you (and me) RECLAIM ourselves for Jesus. We can do this! It's "grow up" time and Paul is going to help us.

> *"Do not let sin control the way you live, do not give in to sinful desires. Do not let any part of your body become an instrument of evil to serve sin. Instead, give yourselves completely to God, for you were dead, but now you have new life. So use your whole*

body as an instrument to do what is right for the glory of God. Sin is no longer your master, for you no longer live under the requirements of the law. Instead, you live under the freedom of God's grace."

ROMANS 6:12

LET'S DO IT!

"Don't copy the behavior and customs of this world, but let God transform you into a new person by changing the way you think. Then you will learn to know God's will for you, which is good and pleasing and perfect."

ROMANS 12:2

"Don't just pretend to love others. Really love them. Hate what is wrong. Hold tightly to what is good. Love each other with genuine affection, and take delight in honoring each other. Never be lazy, but work hard and serve the Lord enthusiastically. Rejoice in our confident hope. Be patient in trouble, and keep on praying. When God's people are in need, be ready to help them. Always be eager to practice hospitality."

ROMANS 12:9-13

"Bless those who persecute you. Don't curse them; pray that God will bless them. Be happy with those who are happy, and weep with those who weep. Live in harmony with each other. Don't be too proud to enjoy the company of ordinary people. And don't think you know it all!"

ROMANS 12:14-16

"Run from sexual sin! No other sin so clearly affects the body as this one does. For sexual immorality is a sin against your own body."

1 CORINTHIANS 6:18

"Be joyful. Grow to maturity. Encourage each other. Live in harmony and peace. Then the God of love and peace will be with you."

2 CORINTHIANS 13:11

"...throw off your old sinful nature and your former way of life, which is corrupted by lust and deception. Instead, let the Spirit renew your thoughts and attitudes. Put on your new nature, created to be like God—truly righteous and holy."

EPHESIANS 4:22-24

"So stop telling lies. Let us tell our neighbors the truth, for we are all parts of the same body. And "don't sin by letting anger control you." Don't let the sun go down while you are still angry..."

EPHESIANS 4:25-26

"Don't use foul or abusive language. Let everything you say be good and helpful, so that your words will be an encouragement to those who hear them. And do not bring sorrow to God's Holy Spirit by the way you live. Remember, he has identified you as his own, guaranteeing that you will be saved on the day of redemption."

EPHESIANS 4:29-30

"Get rid of all bitterness, rage, anger, harsh words, and slander, as well as all types of evil behavior. Instead, be kind to each other, tenderhearted, forgiving one another, just as God through Christ has forgiven you."

EPHESIANS 4:31-32

"Let there be no sexual immorality, impurity or greed among you. Such sins have no place among God's people.

> *Obscene stories, foolish talk, and coarse jokes—these are not for you. Instead let there be thankfulness to God."*
>
> EPHESIANS 5:3-4

> *"Pray in the Spirit at all times and on every occasion. Stay alert and be persistent in your prayers for all believers everywhere."*
>
> EPHESIANS 6:18

> *"Don't be selfish; don't try to impress others. Be humble, thinking of others as better than yourselves. Don't look out only for your own interests, but take an interest in others, too."*
>
> PHILIPPIANS 2:3-4

> *"…Work hard to show the results of your salvation, obeying God with deep reverence and fear. For God is working in you, giving you the desire and the power to do what pleases him."*
>
> PHILIPPIANS 2:12-13

> *"Do everything without complaining and arguing, so that no one can criticize you. Live clean, innocent lives as children of God, shining like bright lights in a world full of crooked and perverse people."*
>
> PHILIPPIANS 2:14-15

> *"Don't worry about anything; instead, pray about everything. Tell God what you need, and thank him for all he has done. Then you will experience God's peace, which exceeds anything we can understand. His peace will guard your heart and minds as you live in Christ Jesus."*
>
> PHILIPPIANS 4:6-7

> *"...Fix your thoughts on what is true, and honorable, and right, and pure, and lovely, and admirable. Think about things that are excellent and worthy of praise."*
>
> PHILIPPIANS 4:8

Whew! Let's be honest. After reading through these, how did you feel? It's one thing to enforce scripture to stand against the enemy. It's another thing to feel like we've just used the scripture to beat ourselves up! Remember, the flesh will always be opposed to the Spirit. (re-read Romans 8) Paul would not have told us to do these things if he didn't do them himself. But Paul also gives us the key to overcoming the power of "self" by deciding who is in control. Will we live by "what we want, think or feel" or will we choose to be controlled and obedient to the Spirit of God? After all, the Spirit of God, who raised Jesus from the dead, lives in you... and in me. (Romans 8:11)

Of course, these scriptures are not a complete list of Paul's imperative sentences, but it's a start. There's more in Colossians, Thessalonians and Timothy! But for now, take one or two of the ones above that really rub your flesh the wrong way, and ask the Holy Spirit to help you overcome! Confess out loud the passages over yourself! Choosing to cooperate with the Holy Spirit, instead of living for ourselves, is a great way to bring wonderful joy to our lives.

Most of the time, we know how we should act towards others and how to be Christlike, yet we have to DO IT! Jesus said,

> *"But even more blessed are all who hear the word of God and put it into practice!"*
>
> LUKE 11:28

An interesting truth is Jesus defeated Satan at the Cross. He conquered once and for all the power of sin and death. He gave US His authority to use against the enemy. But He did not deliver us from our flesh! WE have to BE WILLING and choose to deal with our flesh. So many times I hear people blame so much on "the devil was after me today" or "I've been fighting the devil today." When often times we are giving the devil too much credit over areas in our lives where we are letting our flesh be in control! Remember, the Spirit is opposed to the Flesh and vice versa. Honestly, I despise the devil so much that I don't want to give him credit for ANY negative thing in my life. Be careful about talking too much about the devil, but instead be God-focused and talk more about what God is doing! Again, DO IT! We have to choose those things that lead to holiness. Choose the thoughts that lead to holiness. Choose the words that lead to holiness. Choose the actions that lead to holiness. Would you be willing to choose holiness?

One last scripture:

> *"Oh, that my actions would consistently reflect your decrees! Then I will not be ashamed when I compare my life with your commands. As I learn your righteous regulations, I will thank you by living as I should! I will obey your decrees. Please don't give up on me!"*
>
> PSALM 119:5-8

Today feels like more of a Total Makeover, doesn't it? Oh, but won't the reveal be glorious! We'll look like Jesus! Amen!

CHAPTER EIGHTEEN

Falling In Love...Again

There are two amazing women in the Bible that I can so identify with...Mary and Martha. These women, who are sisters, loved Jesus, yet they had totally different personalities. As we go through their stories, I would imagine the female readers can identify a bit more with these women's emotions than the male readers. Actually, maybe the men can identify, it's just that women tend to be more vocal about how we feel! Ha!

We first meet these ladies in Luke 10:38-42. In just four verses, we can tell a lot about their personalities. Jesus and his disciples entered a village, Bethany, on their way to

Jerusalem, and stopped off for a meal at the home of Martha and Mary. While Martha is preparing this amazing meal, Mary decides to sit and just absorb everything that Jesus is teaching the group. This upsets Martha to the point that she cannot hold her tongue, but complains to Jesus about the lack of help. If I had to guess, this may not have been the first time Martha felt like Mary didn't share in the responsibilities. Otherwise, she would have responded differently. Let's look at this conversation,

> "She (Martha) came to Jesus and said, 'Lord doesn't it seem unfair to you that my sister just sits here while I do all the work? Tell her to come and help me.' But the Lord said to her, 'My dear Martha, you are worried and upset over all these details! There is only one thing worth being concerned about. Mary has discovered it and it will not be taken away from her.'"
>
> LUKE 10:40-42

Yes, I have a feeling Martha has had that "I do all the work around here" feeling many times. She's a "doer" and I bet she was efficient, creative and probably liked to be in charge. I confess, I'm not one who enjoys cooking, but I have Martha tendencies. There is such a struggle on the inside when you like to be in charge and do everything a certain way, yet feel offended when nobody offers to help. The times

I've gotten offended or overly occupied with the task is when I'm nervous about the event, or feel under qualified. No doubt, Martha had prepared many dinner parties, but this wasn't an ordinary guest. Therefore, do you think Martha was nervous, or concerned that her gifts or skills wouldn't be good enough? And when an efficient, organized person starts feeling this way, we tend to shift blame and complain. That way, if for some reason the situation doesn't turn out successful, we can say, "well, I didn't have any help!" or "this was too much of a job for one person!"

Jesus recognizes Martha's frustration and points out that she is way too anxious and upset. In other words, she was focused on the wrong thing. We can be so focused on performing and serving Jesus that we totally miss His presence being there. Martha complaining about Mary wasn't really about Mary. It was about the insecurities coming out in Martha. I think Martha was so obsessed with the job that she forgot who she was serving…that it wasn't about the food, it was about Jesus. Have you been guilty of this? Times when you are a world-class server for the kingdom of God, yet you find yourself complaining to the Lord about all you do. That's when we get out of balance…too much serving and not enough soaking. Jesus had nothing against the wonderful food being prepared…it's just that the spiritual food He was offering was more important.

What I do love about Martha is she doesn't keep it

inside. Yes, she complained, but she went to Jesus instead of complaining to others. Yes, there are times in ministry and serving when we lose focus on why we are serving. That's when we need to go to Jesus and talk to him. Share the hurt, but then be willing to listen and let Him bring you back in balance.

We next read about these two in the Gospel of John 11:1-44 (read), and we find out they have a brother name Lazarus. Lazarus becomes very sick, so the sisters get word to Jesus to please come and help their brother. Jesus has a very close relationship with this family of siblings, yet instead of quickly going to help Lazarus, he does something unexpected…He waits. Jesus knows Lazarus has died, but he lets days pass, then he tells the disciples it's time to go see this family. By the time they arrive in Bethany, Lazarus has been dead for four days. The mourners are at their house and Martha and Mary are heartbroken.

> *"When Martha got word that Jesus was coming, she went to meet him. But Mary stayed in the house."*
>
> JOHN 11:20

What? Based on their personalities, I would think Mary would have been the one to run out to meet Jesus; Mary, the one who sat at His feet. If I put myself in Mary's shoes, I would have been offended…with Jesus. Have you ever felt

Falling In Love...Again

like Mary? You spend time in the Lord's presence, interceding for others, worshipping, and soaking up that quiet time with God. You have the most amazing heart for Jesus, and then something unexpected happens that rocks your world. And your first thought is, "but Lord, I don't understand...I've prayed, served you, fellowshipped with you, studied the Word and you know I'm totally devoted to you...so why Lord, why?"

Let me ask it this way, "Have you ever been mad at God?" OK, I'll be transparent here...yes, I have. I've been very upset with God when I have felt like He could have prevented something and He didn't. The times when the disappointments, or the unexpected happens to where it feels like my foundation in Christ is totally shaken. I can remember being so upset with God one time that I told Him I wasn't going to read the Bible anymore! That, of course, didn't last long! How can you be mad at the only One you know can do something about your situation? Let's see what Mary does.

Jesus reminds Martha that He is the resurrection and the life and she acknowledges that she totally understands that He is the Messiah and the Son of God. Then Martha does something a little odd:

> "Then she (Martha) returned to Mary. She called Mary aside from the mourners and told her, 'The Teacher is here and wants to see you.' So Mary immediately went to him."
>
> JOHN 11:28-29

I cannot find in scripture where Jesus asked to see Mary. My personal observation is this could be a "tell tale sign" that Mary was offended with Jesus, but Martha knew the heart of her sister very well. She knew the only way to get her up and moving was to tell her, "Hey, Jesus wants to see you." That's all it took...Mary immediately gets up and runs to Jesus. She loved Him so much. I love what Mary does when she gets to Him:

> *"When Mary arrived and saw Jesus, she fell at his feet..."*
>
> JOHN 11:32

We read that Jesus raises Lazarus from the dead to strengthen the believers and bring glory to God. But how did this experience really affect Mary and Martha? Let's go to John 12:1-11, (read)

> *"Six days before the Passover celebration began, Jesus arrived in Bethany, the home of Lazarus—the man he had raised from the dead. A dinner was prepared in Jesus' honor. Martha served, and Lazarus was among those who ate with him. Then Mary took a twelve-ounce jar of expensive perfume made from essence of nard, and she anointed Jesus' feet with it, wiping his feet with her hair."*
>
> JOHN 12:1-3

I believe both women had their focus back and grew a stronger love for Jesus. They RECLAIMED how much they loved Him. Martha was serving...not to impress people, not upset and not overly occupied. She was serving Jesus. And Mary...her experience took her worship to a whole new level! She beautifully ministers to Jesus in such an intimate way.

Having a relationship with God means it's just that...a relationship. Yes, we need to always be reverent, and remember that He is God and we are not. Yet there will be times we don't understand His ways and frankly, we may feel hurt, confused, disappointed, offended or mad. If this happens, then RUN to Him. RECLAIM the relationship and talk to Him. Listen to Him, humble yourself and trust Him. It will take your relationship to another level!

"Precious Lord Jesus, I desire for my relationship with You to be the most important relationship I have. I love You Lord and I ask You to forgive me when I have not understood Your ways, or have blamed You for disappointments in my life. Even though I may not understand, I do know that YOU ARE GOOD, and I can trust You. Help me RECLAIM my relationship with You daily and proclaim with confidence that YOU ARE MY GOD! You are my King, Savior, Lord and Friend. Throughout my life, let every experience draw me closer and closer to You. AMEN!"

SECTION FOUR

Would You Be Willing To Rejoice?

Before we begin this new section, let's look back and recap our journey. We began with the subject of **Repentance** and how we can go to God daily to ask for forgiveness of sin, as well as ask for forgiveness on behalf of others and our nation. Repentance brings us back to sweet fellowship with God and turns us from old ways or choices, and allows Him to help us choose His ways.

In the second section we learned how **Receiving** from God cleanses and empowers us from sin by receiving God's forgiveness and power through the precious Holy Spirit. We studied how relationship with God is like a transaction and how we need to be good receivers from Him, instead of trying to change in our own strength.

By getting to know and being filled with the Holy Spirit, we learned in section three the necessity of **Reclaiming** and living with more of a spiritual perspective. We learned we have a spiritual enemy and also, we have a powerful fleshly, sinful nature, yet we can "take back," reclaim our spiritual rights through our authority in Christ, and not just live by letting our feelings dictate our choices.

There may be chapters you want to reread at this point and ask the Lord to help you with any area that continues to be a struggle. I encourage you to lean on the Body of Christ. If you hear in your head at anytime, "I don't want to bother anyone with this," or "nobody will understand," then that is a 100% guarantee that you need to seek out a Christian counselor, pastor, bible study group or Christian friend to help. Don't be an island and think you can do this alone, or fix things by yourself. We are strong as a Body with Jesus Christ as the Head. We don't have time for going solo in life. We need each other! And there is someone who needs YOU and your gifts too!

Let's now talk about **Rejoicing**! That just sounds like it's going to be a happy six chapters, doesn't it? Rejoicing always makes me think about powerful praise music with all of the instruments going full blast! You know by now I love visuals, so close your eyes and picture REJOICING!

(Wait, leave one eye open so you can read too!) See the congregation? Everyone is singing at the top of their lungs, with hands raised high! There is clapping, shouting and yes, some are even dancing! No holding back...everyone leaning in and celebrating Jesus! Do you see it? Reminds me of a Chris Tomlin concert I went to a few years ago...The angels had to have been jealous of the Body of Christ that night! The rejoicing was so loud, it was deafening in such a beautiful way! If I could live in a Christian concert or a sanctuary full of worshipping believers, that would be wonderful! But I can't, and neither can you!

I've always thought that if I were continuously happy, then my rejoicing would sound a lot better in God's ears! Oh, but that's not the kind of rejoicing that changes me. We have to look at rejoicing as more than just a Sunday morning thing, and see it as a "transforming" power in our daily lives. In Romans 5:2-4, Paul shares about rejoicing in a strange way...

> *"Because of our faith, Christ has brought us into this place of undeserved privilege where we now stand, and we confidently and joyfully look forward to sharing God's glory. We can REJOICE too, when we run into problems and trials, for we know that they help us develop endurance. And endurance develops strength of character, and character strengthens our confident hope of salvation."*
>
> ROMANS 5:2-4

I'm all in on that first part about "joyfully looking forward to sharing God's glory," but then he goes the opposite direction and says I can rejoice in problems and trials! OK, that's not natural! In fact, I don't intuitively want to do that! No, without understanding the whole meaning…God's meaning of rejoicing… I will miss the fullness of rejoicing. It's available to not only help me in tough spots…it helps me grow up!!

So what does rejoicing look like? What is it about God that would make me want to rejoice? What kind of rejoicing is biblical? Let's dig deep and see why rejoicing is so powerful!

CHAPTER NINETEEN

Fully Awake

One day I had coffee with two dear friends. One sister in Christ decided to spontaneously pray over me a beautiful prayer. It was one of those prayers that you go back and forth between listening and feeling. You want to listen and hang on every word because you know it was prompted by the Lord and you want to try and remember every word. But you also want to just relax, breathe and feel the prayer...just soak in it, because...again, you know it was prompted by the Lord! Finally, you realize you just have to receive by faith, because it's beyond trying to listen to every word, and beyond trying to feel it all. Spiritual things are like that sometimes; more than what our mind can think and more than what our emotions can feel. So I ended up just saying, "Lord, thank you, I receive and I know you'll bring into remembrance any details I need when the time comes."

The other sister in Christ said, "I believe I have a word for you, so I'll just step out in faith and say it." I encouraged her, "Yes, please tell me." She said two simple words, "FULLY AWAKE." For the rest of the afternoon and on into the next day I just kept thinking "fully awake." Hoping the Lord would show me something new related to rejoicing, I started researching this phrase in the Bible.

Midway through the Gospel of Luke, Chapter 9, I read the story of The Transfiguration (also in Matthew 17 and Mark 9). All three gospels are similar, yet Luke adds a detail to his version, which is very important. In this story, Jesus takes Peter, James and John up to a mountain for a 24-hour prayer trip. While the three are sleeping, Jesus is praying. He suddenly goes from human appearance to looking heavenly, with glowing face and dazzling white clothes. We read, beginning in verse 30,

> *"Suddenly, two men, Moses and Elijah, appeared and began talking with Jesus. They were glorious to see. And they were speaking about his exodus from this world, which was about to be fulfilled in Jerusalem. Peter and the others had fallen asleep. <u>When they woke up</u>, they*

> *saw Jesus' glory and the two men standing with him."*
>
> LUKE 9:30-32

Let me sum up the rest of this amazing experience. Peter sees Moses and Elijah start to leave and he starts babbling, and without thinking suggests building huts for each of them. Don't you love Peter? Have you ever blurted out something rather ridiculous, especially in front of important people? Maybe the pastor of your church, your boss, or new acquaintances? Then you think later, "Why did I say that?" Well, next time it happens, take comfort that you and I are in great company with Peter!

Then a cloud covers the men, and a voice is heard,

> *"This is my son, My Chosen One. Listen to him."*
>
> LUKE 9:35

After the voice stopped, Jesus was transformed back to his human appearance. The story ends by saying,

> *"They didn't tell anyone at that time what they had seen."*
>
> LUKE 9:36

So what in the world does "**Fully Awake** and **Rejoicing**" have to do with this story?

There are a few times in the New Testament that use the word "awake" or "awaken", which in the Greek simply means to "wake up from a sleep, to arouse from sleep, or to become of a sober mind." But in the scripture above, the original Greek word means something a bit different. It's not just being "awake" but "fully awake." It means "**to watch through and to remain awake.**" Now obviously we can't remain awake and never sleep again as long as we have this earthly body, but let's turn on our spiritual thinking and grasp this story.

The disciples didn't just wake up from sleep; they became "fully awake." What they saw was crystal clear. There was no "are we dreaming?" Can you imagine how their minds and emotions were trying to process this? They had nothing to compare it to. They knew exactly who Moses and Elijah were…how? No photographs or "ancestry.com" back then. They saw Jesus unlike they had ever seen Him before. These guys were the choice three that understood more about who Jesus was and about spiritual things more than the other disciples. Yet this brief moment was so spiritual and so indescribable that they chose to not mention it to others. After all, how would they describe it, and even if others believed the story, would they really understand it spiritually?

But God made sure they were "fully awake" to see this supernatural scene and hear His voice. He made them "fully awake" to **watch through the natural and remain**

spiritually awake for the rest of their lives. This experience was prompted by God, but it was more than their minds could understand. These guys had seen miracle after miracle, yet this was beyond their thinking. Just days earlier they had seen Jesus multiply bread and fish to feed 5000 people, but now they weren't just beholding another miracle...they were beholding **His glory.**

God, in His goodness, pulled back a heavenly veil and allowed them to see...FULLY SEE Jesus. They were beholding more than his teaching, wisdom, and miracle-working power. Peter even shares in 2 Peter 1:16-18,

> *"We saw his majestic splendor with our own eyes when he received honor and glory from God the Father. The voice from the majestic glory of God said to him, 'This is my dearly loved Son, who brings me great joy.' We ourselves heard that voice from heaven when we were with him on the holy mountain."*
>
> 2 PETER 1:16-18

Peter is making it clear that they weren't dreaming or seeing a vision. They saw and heard! They were fully awakened to His splendor, magnificence, excellence, majesty, deity, and perfection. Up until this point they just witnessed what Jesus could DO...now God was allowing them to witness who He WAS. Again, NOT by their choice...but by God's choice. And how in the world can you process an experience like that emotionally? Simply put, you can't. You can only REJOICE.

In our relationship with God, He wants us to experience Him in so many ways. Have you ever REJOICED in Him just because He is God and you don't have to understand every detail, every experience or situation? Sometimes I just REJOICE that He is so much more than my thinking and understanding…He is so much more than my feelings and emotions…and I am OK with that. There's a comfort and freedom in knowing He's a big, big God and I can trust Him in the midst of not comprehending everything.

Unfortunately, there are times I get caught up in the facts, what I see, what I hear and what I feel. I can easily shrink God down to my size and totally forget His greatness. I can also be like Peter and come up with some ideas and thoughts that humanize God. "Hey God, I see what's happening here, so let me take things from here and do something!" It's like a kid wanting to help with an adult size project. Oh how He must smile at us with amusement at times! He is so good and so sweet to his children, isn't He? Before we pray I want to share how Jesus prayed to the Father about us just before he was to face death on the cross. Notice what He says about His glory,

"Father, the hour has come. Glorify your Son so he can give glory back to you. For you have given him authority over everyone. He gives eternal life to each one you have given him. And this is the way to have eternal life—to know you, the only true God, and Jesus Christ, the one you sent to earth. I brought glory to you here on earth by completing the work you gave me to do. Now, Father, bring me into the glory we shared before the world began.

I have revealed you to the ones you gave me from this world. They were always yours. You gave them to me, and they have kept your word. Now they know that everything I have is a gift from you, for I have passed on to them the message you gave me. They accepted it and know that I came from you, and they believe you sent me.

My prayer is not for the world, but for those you have given me, because they belong to you. All who are mine belong to you, and you have given them to me, so they bring me glory. Now I am departing from the world; they are staying in this world, but I am coming to you. Holy Father, you have given me your name; now protect them by the power of your name so that they will be united just as we are. During my time here, I protected them by the power of the name you gave me. I guarded them so that not one was lost, except the one headed for destruction, as the Scriptures foretold.

Now I am coming to you. I told them many things while I was with them in this world so they would be filled with my joy. I have given them your word. And the world hates them because they do not belong to the world, just as I do not belong to the world. I'm not asking you to take them out of the world, but to keep them safe from the evil one. They do not belong to this world any more than I do. Make them holy by your truth; teach them your word, which is truth. Just as you sent me into the world, I am sending them into the world. And I give myself as a holy sacrifice for them so they can be made holy by your truth.

I am praying not only for these disciples but also for <u>all</u> who will ever believe in me through their message. I pray that they will all be one, just as you and I are one—as you are in me, Father, and I am in you. And may they be in us so that the world will believe you sent me.

I have given them the glory you gave me, so they may be one as we are one. I am in them and you are in me. May they experience such perfect unity that the world will know that you sent me and that you love them as much as you love me. Father, I want these whom you have given me to be with me where I am. Then they can see all the glory you gave me because you loved me even before the world began!

O righteous Father, the world doesn't know you, but I do; and these disciples know you sent me. I have revealed you to them, and I will continue to do so. Then your love for me will be in them, and I will be in them."

JOHN 17:1-26

"Lord Jesus, help me to be more "fully awake" to who You are. Thank You that You desire for me to pray and ask You to help, change, and be a part of every area of my life, but Jesus, I desire to see and know more of YOU. Not for what You can do, but for who You are. I know that just Your presence changes me. By faith, I ask You to fill me with a fresh desire to know You more and experience Your love for me... more and more. Even though I may not always understand in my thoughts or emotions, I REJOICE that You are God, and You are good! I join with the angels and REJOICE in your glory! AMEN!"

CHAPTER TWENTY

Shall We Dance?

Years ago my mother introduced me to her new pastor's wife, Julie. I'll never forget laying eyes on this tall, slender, beautiful woman for the first time. Although I had grown up in church, I actually met Jesus in 1993 and was filled with His Spirit. I now understood the difference between knowing about Jesus and having a relationship with Jesus. So when I met Julie in 1997, I was growing and experiencing the Lord in so many ways. I was going to Christian conferences, regularly reading my bible, and going to an amazing bible study. But seeing Julie was a brand new experience for me... when I saw her, I saw Jesus. It's a little hard to describe, but

I could physically see in her eyes, her face, and in her smile that she was full of the Lord. And she hadn't even said a word to me yet. He was just so "present" with her. I knew she was intimate with Him and He was priority in her life. Have you ever met anyone like that?

When I spoke to her and she spoke back, there was an immediate connection. It was like Jesus was introducing us and made us instant friends. I have to admit; I didn't care about where she was from, how she grew up, and didn't even ask about her testimony. I just wanted to know, "How are you so in love with Jesus?"

Soon after meeting Julie, we scheduled a day to get to know each other at her house. As soon as we got our children playing together, Julie started talking about the Lord. We walked in her living room area and she turned on some praise music. Then she said something that completely caught me off guard... "Come on Mary Jo, let's dance before the Lord!"

Uhhhhhh, what? Dance? Now I love to dance, and 80's disco music was my favorite, but she was suggesting something really weird in my mind. I grew up with hymnals and a pipe organ, so I just couldn't imagine what she wanted us to do! Before I could even say, "Now wait a minute," she grabbed my hands and all of a sudden I felt incredibly awkward. I had no idea what to do, so I mostly watched her. Julie's arms were raised up high and she was twirling so gracefully, like a five-year-old little girl wanting to impress her daddy. She had the biggest smile on her face and it was as if she was overflowing with pure, unashamed joy!

Honestly, I wasn't much of a participant that day on the dance floor. That was an expression of rejoicing that was foreign to me. Yet on the drive back home, I talked to the Lord about it. "Lord, I don't understand and I wasn't very comfortable, but I love you and I want to be willing to worship, praise and rejoice in You and for You." Since that day, I admit I have turned on Christian music and danced before the Lord in my home. And I love it!

In 2008, my friend Julie, her husband and children had a fatal car accident. All four were in the presence of the Lord within a split second. I remember hearing the news and being totally shocked. As soon as I cried out to the Lord, I saw the most beautiful sight in my mind. Julie was before the King of Kings. She was beholding the One she had served with her whole heart. And yes, she was dancing for her audience of One. As tragic as the accident was, I knew there was nowhere else Julie would want to be. She was home.

I hope this doesn't sound callus, but I didn't shed any more tears for Julie. She had such kingdom focus that this world paled in her eyes. Yes, Julie was an amazing wife, mother, mentor and friend to so many, but her sights were on Heaven and Jesus. She knew this life was quick compared to eternity. She was a woman devoted to serving, praying, teaching and encouraging believers to get out of their comfort zone...because she knew there was more to God than the box we tend to put Him in. This chapter is by no means about dancing before the Lord, but it is about a "victory dance."

I called a dear friend of mine, who had also been mentored by Julie, and I asked him, "Why do you think Julie rejoiced?" He thought about it and said, "She knew the battle was won!" He compared her to a great football coach; a coach who knew the game, how to instruct the players, how to encourage and how to work hard, yet, knew that the game was already won before you played. Yes, you have to practice during the week, and you have to prepare for the game, but wouldn't your attitude and the way you treat your players be different if you already knew you were going to win? Yes, there would be mistakes, you would take some hard hits, and in the natural it may look like there's no way to win, but your sights aren't on what you see...your confidence is in the truth...Victory.

In 2 Chronicles 20, King Jehoshaphat was facing some enemy opponents. He was terrified at the news of the attack that was coming to the Israelite army. Yet, he feared God more than the enemy armies. He knew his God was mighty, so he had his troops and the people pray and fast. He prayed,

> "O Lord, God of our ancestors, you alone are the God who is in heaven. You are ruler of all the kingdoms of the earth. You are powerful and mighty; no one

> *can stand against you!...We can cry out to you to save us, and you will hear us and rescue us!"*
>
> 2 CHRONICLES 20:6,9

King Jehoshaphat reminded himself and the people who God was and where he and his troops needed to focus their attention. He didn't exactly know how the attack would play out, but he knew he first had to remind himself of the track record of his God. While the people prayed, the Lord spoke through one of the men and he said,

> *"This is what the Lord says: Do not be afraid! Don't be discouraged by this mighty army, for the battle is not yours, but God's. Tomorrow, march out against them....But you will not even need to fight. Take your positions; then stand still and watch the Lord's victory. He is with you, O people of Judah and Jerusalem. Do not be afraid or discouraged. Go out against them tomorrow, for the Lord is with you!"*
>
> 2 CHRONICLES 20:15-17

They had to show up for the game and play the opponent. They had to suit up and face the enemy. But God had already said, "My battle, not yours." So the king leads this army in an unusual way. The first string of defense was not the mightiest warriors of the army...no, instead he leads off with the singers! Can you imagine the scene? A group of singers are leading the troops! They are REJOICING with their voices, singing praises and celebrating the victory!

> *"Give thanks to the Lord; his faithful love endures forever!"*
>
> 2 CHRONICLES 20:21

There's nothing solemn about this bunch! In my mind I picture about 1000 Julie's walking toward the enemy! Hands lifted high! Dancing! Shouting! Singing! This confused the enemy so bad, they started fighting among themselves! The only job left for God's army was to pick up the plunder, which the abundance took three days to collect! Then an even bigger celebration broke out!

> *"They marched into Jerusalem to the music of harps, lyres, and trumpets and they proceeded to the Temple of the Lord. When all the surrounding kingdoms heard that the Lord himself had fought against the enemies of Israel, the fear of God came over them. So Jehoshaphat's kingdom was at peace, for his God had given him rest on every side."*
>
> 2 CHRONICLES 20:28-30

REJOICING in the victory BEFORE anything happens is a powerful thing! It shifts the focus to God. It says, "I don't know how this will play out God, but I give you the battle, and I trust You."

Through trials, suffering, adversity and disappointments, Julie was doing victory dances because she cooperated and had faith in the promises of God. She knew scripture and knew how the story ends. She didn't have to know all the details or how things would play out...she just knew God was God, and never doubted. Why did she leave this world so early? Why a tragic car accident? I have no idea. But I do know what she's doing this very minute...dancing!

If you and I were chosen by the King to be the "front line" how would we express REJOICING? Well my friend, we ARE the front line. Let's tune up, stretch, and dress out! Let's make the Coach proud he put us in the game. We come...we come to win!

"Lord Jesus, teach me how to REJOICE in You that goes beyond just a bowed head and whispered prayers. Open my heart and mind to the truth that I can REJOICE because I serve a victorious King! I confess and receive that I have the freedom to worship, sing and REJOICE before King Jesus because He is worthy. Praise You Lord!"

CHAPTER TWENTY ONE

The Warfare Of Worship

In the last chapter we read about King Jehoshaphat and the praise and worship singers who led the Israelite army to a victory over the enemy. Remember during their fasting and prayer, the Lord gave one man a word to speak. Let's look back at one of the scriptures from 2 Chronicles 20 and see who this man was,

> "As all the men of Judah stood before the Lord with their little ones, wives, and children, the Spirit of the Lord came upon <u>one of the men</u> standing there. His name was Jahaziel son of Zechariah, son of Benaiah, son of Jeiel, son

of Mattaniah, <u>a Levite who was a descendant of Asaph</u>."

2 CHRONICLES 20:13-14

I love it when the Word of God gives us a history lesson. This man, Jahaziel, spoke an important word to the king and everyone present. And it wasn't based on his wisdom, experience or strategic know-how. He spoke because the Holy Spirit gave him the words. This wasn't just any man. We are given some ancestry information on this man, which narrows down to...<u>a Levite who was a descendant of Asaph</u>. Why is this important to know?

First of all, there were twelve tribes of Israel established from the beginning...all the way back to Genesis. These tribes came from the twelve sons of Jacob. One of those sons was Levi, which from this son came the tribe of the Levites. One of the many responsibilities a Levite had was the anointing of worship. This role of "ministers of music" was not for just listening to pretty instruments or song, but for warfare. The Jewish people knew that REJOICING in the God of Abraham, Isaac and Jacob, was not a quiet, passive or timid job. For example, in Psalm 100,

"Shout with joy to the Lord, all the earth! Worship the Lord with gladness. Come before him, singing with joy"

PSALM 100:1-2

David writes in Psalm 101,

> "I will sing of your love and justice, Lord.
> I will praise you with songs."
>
> PSALM 101:1

And in Psalm 150,

> *Praise the LORD! Praise God in his sanctuary; praise him in his mighty heaven! Praise him for his mighty works; praise his unequaled greatness! Praise him with a blast of the ram's horn; praise him with the lyre and harp! Praise him with the tambourine and dancing; praise him with strings and flutes! Praise him with a clash of cymbals; praise him with loud clanging cymbals. Let everything that breathes sing praises to the LORD! Praise the LORD!*
>
> PSALM 150:1-6

There is nothing quiet in these verses. In fact, I wonder if this was the sound as the singers and musicians were walking towards the enemy in the last chapter! Bold, confident in the Lord, with their focus on a great God! Now that's a very important job to have in the kingdom and God required that job be held by a Levite.

In 1 Chronicles 15, King David was moving the Ark of the Covenant to Jerusalem and he appointed a group of Levites to lead the way with songs of REJOICING with skilled worshippers and musicians. In this group was a man named, Asaph. In 1 Chronicles 16:4-5,

> *"David appointed the following Levites to lead the people in worship before the Ark of the Lord to invoke his blessings, to give thanks, to praise the Lord, the God of Israel. <u>Asaph</u>, the leader of this group, sounded the cymbals."*
>
> 1 CHRONICLES 16:4-5

Asaph was a young man when he began working for the king. Can you imagine being a young man and chosen to be the director of music for the king of Israel? Let's think about this and how Asaph must have felt. He knew his heritage was being a man of warfare through the power of music, so he didn't take his job lightly. Quite the contrary, if certain guidelines were not met and the presence of God was not approached a particular way…the Spirit of God would strike a man dead. So, although this position involved a job of singing, playing instruments and REJOICING before the Lord, it was as much a military job as well. This position required relationship with God, discernment and walking in the fear of the Lord. There was no room for sloppy preparation, doing the job halfway, or winging it!

Asaph worked closely with David as his director of

music. From the history of David, we know he was passionate about music, worship and was also skilled with playing instruments. So for Asaph, this was a dream job. David was Asaph's hero, mentor, and friend. Not only working for the king, but being like-minded in executing the very best praise and worship for God possible in lyrics, collaboration of instruments, vocals, backgrounds, and melody. So when David perhaps would say, "Asaph, I have written a song of thanksgiving to the Lord! Would you produce it and make it outstanding?" Wow! What an honor! Then Asaph would gather the band members together and they would go to the studio, and work all hours into the night and give their very best! OK, this is a modern version, but you get my point.

David and Asaph understood each other when it came to REJOICING in the Lord. Why? Because Asaph had a relationship with God too. David knew Asaph was there not to just please him, but to please God. David could trust Asaph because Asaph lived to glorify God, no matter what. As the years went by, Asaph's sons and grandsons were trained as well. The other appointed Levities also had sons, so in other words, there were many families working for the king for the purpose of worshipping God as fully as possible...288 musicians in all! (1 Chronicles 25) Wow! Now that's a band!

Asaph worked for David the whole forty years he was king of Israel. What a journey of seeing battles won, growth of a kingdom and witnessing the goodness of the

Lord through this chosen king. And what joy to know that you participated in bringing glory, honor, and praise to the Lord through REJOICING with music. But then a change in leadership happens.

David's son, Solomon, becomes king and slowly things change. Asaph continues to work in his position even after his beloved king and friend passes away, but it's not the same. Although the Temple is built, direction starts to change in Israel. Solomon doesn't write songs like his dad, his focus shifts to a more materialistic lifestyle, and the kingdom becomes more about pleasure and power than devotion to God. Solomon hires different kinds of employees and administration, which allows pagan practices in the kingdom. Things spiral downhill quickly. Solomon even reflects about this later in life in the book of Ecclesiastes.

Asaph's dreams are shattered and Israel divides. A civil war breaks out and lives are lost. Asaph loses family members and total devastation and horror is the new normal. The Temple is destroyed, and the hopes of a "prophesied Messiah" through David's son are dead. This was not what Asaph was expecting. At his old age, this was not how he thought he would live out his final days. Did you know Asaph wrote Psalm 50, and 73 through 83? Let's see how he handled bitterness, distress, disappointment and tragedy.

- Asaph knew God required a thankful heart.

  "Make thankfulness your sacrifice to God, and keep the vows you made to the Most High. Then call on me when you are in trouble, and I will rescue you, and you will give me glory....But giving thanks is a sacrifice that truly honors me. If you keep to my path, I will reveal to you the salvation of God."

  PSALM 50:14-15, 23

- When Asaph struggled with bitterness and envy, he refocused his attention to God so he could clearly see the greatness of God.

  "My health may fail, and my spirit may grow weak, but God remains the strength of my heart; he is mine forever....But as for me, how good it is to be near God! I have made the Sovereign Lord my shelter, and I will tell everyone about the wonderful things you do."

  PSALM 73:26, 28

- Asaph knew God was a God of justice and He knew how to handle wickedness. He knew how to engage his will!

> *"It is God alone who judges; he decides who will rise and who will fall....But as for me, I will always proclaim what God has done; I will sing praises to the God of Jacob. For God says, "I will break the strength of the wicked, but I will increase the power of the godly."*
>
> PSALM 75:7,9-10

I have selected just a few verses, but I encourage you to read all of these Psalms of Asaph. He was a man just like us! We have his writings to help us understand, turn and overcome disappointments and tragedy through the power of REJOICING in God. He knew what it was like to lose sleep over pain and distress. He understood feeling rejected by the Lord and feeling lost and confused. He experienced devastation and heartache. Yet, Asaph understood the power, healing, and warfare of REJOICING!

Asaph never stopped singing. He knew every love song to God was also a mighty weapon against the enemy. He never stopped proclaiming the name of the Lord. He never stopped trusting God. No matter who was king, he stayed focused on THE KING and continued to REJOICE!

"Almighty God, teach me how to be a skilled worshipper. No matter what my musical talent is, I choose to be a REJOICER, because You are my KING. Teach me to use my voice to sing praises to You. Teach me how to bring

The Warfare Of Worship

worship and thanksgiving to You as a gift and love song to You. Fill my heart to overflowing with gratitude, in spite of circumstances, disappointment or detours in my life. God, You see the bigger picture; therefore, I choose to put my faith in You. Give me the heart of a Levite and teach me to proclaim in confidence and boldness...I AM VICTORIOUS IN JESUS CHRIST! AMEN!"

CHAPTER TWENTY TWO

Forever A Student

There are those who are academically minded and those of us who are not. My oldest daughter attended nursing school, but decided being a nurse wasn't her call. Nevertheless, she loved taking nursing classes, studying the medical books, the terminology and learning all about the body. She finished the semester with an "A", but knew this was not her path. I can remember her telling me, "I would love to continue nursing school, just to learn all the information."

I replied, "Yeah, and avoid taking tests!"

She quickly disagreed, "Oh no, I would want to take all the tests, because I would want to see how much I had learned."

I unashamedly admit there is nothing in me that would want to go back to school, especially to take the tests! This kind of twisted thinking definitely makes her like her father's side of the family. I do have to admit, as she was learning all about the parts of the head, arms and back, I would get some excellent massages out of her studying. I would even tell her she was wrong and make her do it again. She knew she was right, but she humored me. Hey, I thought I was an effective study buddy.

Although school is not always enjoyable…increasing knowledge, being skilled and yes, taking the tests are very important. It's important in day to day life, in our career paths, in learning a special skill, and it is crucial in our spiritual life as well. We want to always and forever be a student of the Word of God. And as we continuously increase our knowledge, we begin to practice and apply what we have learned.

In the four gospels Jesus was referred to many times as "teacher." When he chose those first twelve men to be his disciples, they immediately became students. He taught them both verbally and by example, and yes, they also took spiritual tests…over and over.

For this chapter, let's take the posture of a student and learn. My favorite example of a great student is Peter.

In 2 Peter 1:2-4, Peter writes,

Forever A Student

> "May God give you more and <u>more grace and peace as you grow in your knowledge</u> of God and Jesus our Lord. By his <u>divine power</u>, God has given us everything we need <u>for living a godly life</u>. We have received all of this <u>by coming to know him</u>, the one who called us to himself by means of his marvelous glory and excellence. And because of his glory and excellence, he has given us <u>great and precious promises</u>. These are the promises that enable you to <u>share his divine nature</u> and <u>escape the world's corruption caused by human desires</u>."
>
> 2 PETER 1:2-4

There is something conditional about this sentence. I have a part is this relationship with Jesus...to get to know Him. As I increase more knowledge of Him, this anointed knowledge activates my faith to believe that through Him I have access to more and more grace and peace.

The best way we can get to know Jesus better and better is through the Bible. There is no way we can apply the benefits of his death, resurrection, promises and power, if we don't know about them!

Verses 5 through 7 says,

> "In view of all this, <u>make every effort</u> to respond to God's promises. Supplement your faith with a generous provision of <u>moral excellence</u>, and moral excellence with <u>knowledge</u>, and knowledge with <u>self-control</u>, and self-

> *control with <u>patient endurance</u>, and patient endurance with <u>godliness</u>, and godliness with <u>brotherly affection</u>, and brotherly affection with <u>love for everyone</u>."*
>
> 2 PETER 1:5-7

Again, there's conditions…we have to make an effort and we have to apply them. God's promises are available, yet we have to respond to them. How? By faith in God's promises by speaking them and believing them. I want to be a participant in God's promises, don't you? So what are the benefits again of getting to know Jesus better and better? Let's go back to verses 2-4,

- More grace
- More peace
- Divine power to live a godly life
- Great and precious promises
- Share His divine nature
- Escape world's corruption caused by human desire

I can use all of those in my life! By making an effort and applying God's promises, Peter tells me in verses 5-7 what it will produce in me (Read these verses again):

- **Moral excellence** (choosing purity and virtue because I know Him)

- **Knowledge of God** (relationship knowing Him more and more)
- **Self-control** (because I know it pleases Him)
- **Patient endurance** (because I know He is patient with me)
- **Godliness** (because I want to be like Him)
- **Brotherly affection** (love for my brothers and sisters in Christ as family)
- **Love for everyone** (affection or genuine love for everyone...the way Christ loves)

I would like to point out something very important in the seven characteristics above. Look at them as steps, with moral excellence being the first step. One LEADS to the next, which LEADS to the next. We have to start with leading a life with pure hearts and minds. Paul also teaches,

> *"If you keep yourself pure, you will be a special utensil for honorable use. Your life will be clean, and you will be ready for the Master to use you for every good work. Run from anything that stimulates youthful lusts. Instead, pursue righteous living, faithfulness, love, and peace. Enjoy the companionship of those who call on the Lord with pure hearts."*
>
> 2 TIMOTHY 2:21-22

We have to choose to guard our minds and hearts against sin and lust in order to have a better relationship with God. Why? Because He is pure and holy. We get to choose to separate ourselves in our thoughts, behaviors and words to be clean for the Master's use.

This act of our will, with the help of the Holy Spirit, gives us desire to choose self-control to please and be like Him. Then we will learn and walk out patient endurance, because without it we can't go to the next step of godliness, which grows into genuine love...the Christ kind of love He wants us to pour out to others.

One of my frequent prayers is, "Lord, help me love people the way You do." Mary Jo's love is OK, but God's love through Mary Jo is different. To be totally honest, I don't want to "fake love." You know what I mean? The kind of love that looks like love, but has no authenticity or heart in it. Loving people is not just a feeling. For love to change lives, we have to be filled with God's love. It's difficult for me to love people when I haven't spent time with God, if I'm impatient, or not exercising self-control. Hey, I've tried! Doesn't work! Remember, we are students learning from the best teacher...the Holy Spirit. We also have the grace of repentance and taking "tests" again...Praise God!

2 Peter 1:8 also confirms why building these characteristics are so important. Here is a wonderful goal:

> *"The more you grow like this, the <u>more productive and useful</u> you will be in your knowledge of our Lord Jesus Christ."*
>
> 2 PETER 1:8

It takes the knowledge of Jesus in your head and in your heart to become a vessel useful and productive for God. Every day is an opportunity to grow and know Him better and better. Logically, this also means if I choose to avoid reading the Bible, choose not to grow in relationship with Him and never get to know Him, well....I can also be ineffective and unproductive in my knowledge and purpose for the Kingdom of God. Does this mean God will love me less? Of course not. But it does mean I forfeit many blessings, opportunities and promises that God intended for me to have. More importantly, I miss out on getting to know my Lord and Savior, the one who gave His life for me. I miss out on a relationship with the creator of the universe and the one I will meet face to face one day.

> *"But those who fail to develop in this way are shortsighted or blind, forgetting that they have been cleansed from their old sins."*
>
> 2 PETER 1:9

Hey, I don't want to go backwards, do you? Let's never

forgot what God has done for us! We have an amazing privilege to be able to read, study, memorize, and share the Word of God! REJOICE! Let's look at what the Apostle Paul said about knowledge in Philippians 1:9-11 and Colossians 1:9-10,

> "I pray that your lives will overflow more and more, and that you will keep on <u>growing in knowledge and understanding</u>. For I want you to <u>understand what really matters</u>, so that you may live pure and blameless lives until the day of Christ's return. May you always be filled with the fruit of your salvation--the righteous character produced in your life by Jesus Christ-- for this will bring much glory and praise to God."
>
> PHILIPPIANS 1:9-11

> "We ask God to give you a <u>complete understanding</u> of what he wants to do in your lives, and we ask him to make you wise with spiritual wisdom. Then the way you live will always honor and please the Lord, and you will continually do good, kind things for others. All the while, you will <u>learn to know</u> God better and better."
>
> COLOSSIANS 1:9-10

Paul, a scholar and brilliant man, knew that knowledge,

Forever A Student

insight and understanding God was the way to discern and understand what really matters in life. Without knowledge of the Word of God, we would have no idea what God's opinions, desires or instructions are, therefore, we would have no guidelines or wisdom to develop godly lives. We would be easily tempted to just let the guidelines of the world dictate our choices, which would be opposed to God's standards. We would easily live by how we FEEL, and decide that must be what God FEELS too, instead of going by the scriptures. No way around it...growing in knowledge of the Bible matters.

If today is about being a student of the Word...well, having a little homework "at your own pace" applies. I challenge you to spend time reading Psalm 119 and pay special attention the benefits of reading God's Word. You may see words like "instructions, laws, commandments, decrees, regulations, ways, precepts, promise, or principles." Connect the benefit with those words. I'll start you out with verse 1:

> *"Joyful are people of integrity, who follow the instructions of the Lord. Joyful are those who obey his laws and search for him with all their hearts."*
>
> PSALM 119:1

(Benefit of knowing and obeying God's Word = JOY!)

Let's try another one! How about verse 9?

> *"How can a young person stay pure?*
> *By obeying your <u>word</u>."*
>
> PSALM 119:9

There is a connection between the Word of God and walking a life of purity. But without the Word of God, we wouldn't know this or how the power of the Word can help keep us stay pure in body, mind and heart.

I challenge you to go through Psalm 119 and write down the benefits of studying and being obedient to God's word.

One last revelation about Psalm 119, I'd like to share. As you look at the synonyms for the Word...regulations, laws, commandments, decrees, promises, and instructions, etc. also think about ALL of these represent one person...Jesus.

> *"So the Word became human (flesh)*
> *and made his home among us."*
>
> JOHN 1:14

In other words, because the Word became flesh in the person of Jesus Christ, you can just substitute these words for the name of "Jesus!" Jesus IS the Word! Every verse in Psalm 119 points us to Jesus! Just replace with Jesus! For example, verse 1,

> *"Joyful are people of integrity, who follow Jesus. Joyful are those who obey Jesus and search for Jesus with all their hearts."*
>
> PSALM 119:1

How about verse 9?

> *"How can a young person stay pure? By obeying Jesus."*
>
> PSALM 119:9

That makes the Word of God so relational! All scripture points to Jesus!

I love that rewards, blessings and benefits come with being a good student! What a wonderful teacher we serve! Let's look at one last scripture from the Old Testament.

> *"No, O people, the Lord has told you what is good, and this is what he <u>requires</u> of you: to do what is right, to love mercy, and to walk humbly with your God."*
>
> MICAH 6:8

The Hebrew meaning of the word **"requires"** in this verse means: <u>to seek with care, to consult, to practice, to study, to seek with application.</u> Sounds pretty academic doesn't it? Oh, if doing the right thing, loving mercy, and being humble would just fall on us automatically!!! But these character traits do not…they have to be studied, practiced and applied. But oh, doesn't it make our hearts sweeter!!

Have you ever thanked God for His Word? Have you ever REJOICED because you hold God's Word in your hand and in your heart? Let's start today!

"Father God, Thank You so much for Your written Word!

I REJOICE that I can know You through the pages of scripture!

I REJOICE that the Bible changes my thoughts and changes my heart!

I REJOICE that the Bible transforms me to think and sound like You!

I REJOICE that I am a student of the Word of God to learn, apply and live out Your scriptures in my life!

I REJOICE that by knowing the Bible, I will know YOU!

In Jesus Name, AMEN!"

CHAPTER TWENTY THREE

The Beautiful Body Of Christ

One of the things I REJOICE to the Lord about is the Body of Christ. I truly believe I have been blessed with the most amazing believers as family and friends. When I think about how I met some of these friends, I remember meeting them just like it was yesterday. Then oddly, there are some friends that I just can't remember the time or place we first met… it seems they were always just…there. What I do remember are "God-times" with friends. Moments when I needed them or they needed me and Jesus showed up and turned things around for good. Moments where we sharpened each other like iron, or just needed a hug of encouragement. We were never meant to be islands in this life. Jesus was all about relationships, therefore shouldn't we?

There is a remarkable couple we are introduced to in the Book of Acts, Chapter 18. This couple moved to Corinth after Caesar made the decision to deport all Jews from Rome. We don't know their age, but we do know they were tentmakers. So not only did they have to pick up and move, they also had to reestablish their business in a new city. Moving is hard, and starting over is hard, but this couple had a relationship with God. This unexpected disruption in life for this husband-and-wife team was about to become an unexpected blessing! God handpicked them to meet someone very special...The Apostle Paul.

From the moment of Paul's conversion, it seems he was moving and shaking everywhere he went. This man was getting pure teaching straight from the Holy Spirit. There wasn't an ounce of timidity in Paul, just power-packed boldness. God took this brilliant, outspoken, wildly passionate man, who was persecuting Christians.... and transformed him into a brilliant, outspoken, wildly passionate man on fire for Jesus! He went from synagogue to synagogue and preached to the Jews that the Messiah had come and His name was Jesus. Some converted and some didn't. Some became followers and some attacked Paul in rage of his preaching. He was publicly beaten, mobbed and imprisoned on many occasions. Nevertheless, Paul, full of the Holy Spirit, was traveling city to city, country to country, proclaiming the Good News.

When Paul arrived in Corinth, he met this Jewish, tent-making couple, Aquila and Priscilla. This was a divine friendship appointment, so much so, that Paul moved in with them. Being a skilled tent maker as well, Paul began working with this couple to make a living, while he continued to preach.

We don't know if Aquila and Priscilla had heard about Paul, or about the extent of their knowledge of the Good News of Jesus Christ, but we do know they bonded with Paul. Can you imagine someone like Paul moving into your home? Just hearing his testimony about how Jesus met him on the road to Damascus would be life-changing. You get to hear about his missionary journeys and how the power of God opened jail cell doors, delivered people from evil spirits and how he stood up to city officials with words of truth. And every night you get to step into the presence of God when Paul opens his mouth to pray. This couple was being mentored by one of the most amazing followers of Jesus the world would ever know. When Aquila and Priscilla laid down in their bed at night, I wonder if they looked at each other and smiled or laughed saying, "And we thought having to leave Rome was a bad thing!"

Relationships should never be one-way streets. If they are, then it's an unhealthy relationship that will not grow.

Aquila and Priscilla needed Paul in their lives, but I believe Paul needed them. Paul trusted this couple. They nurtured him, loved him, cared for him and prayed for him. It was one of those friendships where you instantly bond and you know no matter how long you are together or how long you are apart, you are bonded in Christ for eternity.

We know through scripture that Paul was a single man, so I also believe having a strong godly woman in his life was important to Paul. While sitting around the dinner table, I can just hear Paul and Aquila talking, then Paul turning to say, "Priscilla, what do you think?" Then she would present a perspective mixed with wisdom and insight. And I believe these men listened to her with the utmost respect. She was an important part of this powerful team who God was molding to set sail on more missionary journeys.

For a year and a half Paul lived in Corinth, and when it was time to leave and go to Syria, he took Aquila and Priscilla with him. They weren't just companions; they represented so much more to Paul. They were his prayer partners, a source of strength, and trusted allies. In Acts, chapter 18, we get a small window into the benefits of the relationships with Aquila and Priscilla.

During a stop-off in Ephesus, a Jew named Apollos was preaching about Jesus. This young man was eloquent, enthusiastic and accurate in preaching, except he only knew about being baptized in water for the repentance of sin, or commonly known as "John's baptism." After preaching to an audience, Aquila and Priscilla took him aside, mentored him and shared about the baptism of the Holy Spirit. Because this couple cared enough to share MORE with this gifted preacher, Apollos went from boldly sharing, to sharing through the power of the Holy Spirit; therefore many came to the Lord.

Aquila and Priscilla were also a couple that opened their home to bible studies. Have you ever known a couple like this? I have. This unique type of couple opens their home to the hurting with warm hearts and a warm meal. They will stay up to all hours of the night praying over someone needing deliverance. They encourage, embrace and use their words to shower someone who has never felt unconditional love. They probably never lock their door at night, just in case someone needs a safe place to spend the night. After all, they trust in the protection of the Lord, so they don't walk in fear. They pour out and sacrifice their lives for others and when God moves and miracles happen, they REJOICE at what God has done! This kind of believer is mentioned in Joel 2 and Acts 2:18,

"In those days I will pour out my spirit
even on my servants —men and women
alike—and they will prophesy."

JOEL 2:29 & ACTS 2:18

Through many travels and experiences, Paul continued to move on and had to part with his faithful friends…his prayer warriors. In Romans 16:3-5 Paul writes,

> *"Give my greetings to Priscilla and Aquila, my co-workers in the ministry of Christ Jesus. In fact, they once risked their lives for me. I am thankful to them, and so are all the Gentile churches. Also give my greetings to the church that meets in their home."*
>
> ROMANS 16:3-5

This dynamic duo risked their very lives for Paul. Why? Because they knew he was God's chosen to take the gospel to not only Jews, but everyone else in the world (Gentiles). Paul loved them so much and was so thankful for them, that I bet ALL of the new churches he started throughout his journey knew the names, Aquila and Priscilla.

Can't you hear Paul say something like, "Let's lift up a prayer of thanksgiving to my faithful friends, Aquila and Priscilla. If it wasn't for them, I wouldn't be here to share the Good News with you. It's these kinds of disciples that make it possible for me to do what Jesus has called me to do!"(Mary Jo's version)

In fact, these kinds of believers should be all believers. There should be characteristics of Aquila and Priscilla in all of us who confess Jesus as Lord. We should be a Body of

Christ that Paul describes in 1 Corinthians 12:4-6,

> *"There are different kinds of spiritual gifts, but the same Spirit is the source of them all. There are different kinds of service, but we serve the same Lord. God works in different ways, but it is the same God who does the work in all of us."*
>
> 1 CORINTHIANS 12:4-6

Paul continued to describe the workings of the Body of Christ and compared it to how human parts work together in a body. We can't all be eyes...or ears...or hands. The body has many parts and just like God created the many, many parts of the human body to work together, He created the Body of Christ to flow in harmony together. Paul also knew that even though he was a "mouth" and was the person in the spotlight, the people behind the scenes who pray, organize, coordinate, work, set up, take down, etc. are crucial. I think when Paul penned this portion of scripture; he reflected and REJOICED over people that God had placed in his life, in different locations, different churches and even just in traveling from point A to point B. He acknowledged these priceless saints by saying in verses 22-27,

> *"In fact, some parts of the body that seem weakest and least important are actually the most necessary. And*

> the parts we regard as less honorable are those we clothe with the greatest care. So we carefully protect those parts that should not be seen, while the more honorable parts do not require this special care. So God has put the body together such that extra honor and care are given to those parts that have less dignity. This makes for harmony among the members, so that all the members care for each other. If one part suffers, all the parts suffer with it, and if one part is honored, all the parts are glad. All of you together are Christ's body, and each of you is part of it."
>
> 1 CORINTHIANS 12:22-27

Remember Apollos? He had an amazing following of believers and instead of seeing him as competition, Paul was grateful for his gifts! He knew that he was another ambassador for Christ, just like him. And Paul knew that it wasn't about name recognition or fame.

> "After all, who is Apollos? Who is Paul? We are only God's servants through whom you believed the Good News. Each of us did the work the Lord gave us. I planted the seed in your hearts, and Apollos watered it, but it was God who made it grow. It's not important who does the planting, or who does the watering. What's important is that God makes the seed grow."
>
> 1 CORINTHIANS 3:5-9

The Beautiful Body Of Christ

Today, let us REJOICE in the Body of Christ! Let's praise God for the many gifts and talents we have as a body and how we need each other. Let's sow seeds of faith, hope and love! Let's pray for a harvest of souls! We are the BODY OF CHRIST and we are BEAUTIFUL!

> *"The godly people in the land are my true heroes! I take pleasure in them!"*
>
> PSALM 16:3

"Lord, thank You so much for the Body of Christ! I REJOICE in the men and women You have placed in my life to witness, share, teach and love. I also ask that You help me to be a bold follower, willing to share the Good News with others. Give me a servant's anointing like Aquila and Priscilla to also support those who stand and are a voice to Christ. Praise you Lord Jesus for being the Head of this beautiful body of believers. Help me, Holy Spirit, to never be an island in my walk, but to seek out support from other believers. In Jesus' Name, AMEN!"

CHAPTER TWENTY FOUR

Shhhhhhh!

In deciding what to write in the final chapter on rejoicing, many topics crossed my mind...Rejoicing in God's kindness, grace, love, generosity, patience, or discipline. Trying to decide on why we rejoice in God is like trying to choose a favorite star in the sky. We rejoice because every aspect of God is worth rejoicing about. He created us...Rejoice! He allowed us to wake up this morning...Rejoice! He is the author and finisher of our faith....Rejoice! He knows all things and sees all things...Rejoice! He is NOT like me and He is NOT like you...haha, yes REJOICE!

I would like to confess that there's a principle of

fellowshipping with God that I have trouble with...Silence. We have the ability by the precious person of the Holy Spirit to hear from God. To actually receive direction, comfort, peace and faith from the God of the Universe, yet I confess I can be a terrible listener. Especially, if I am upset about something, or sad about a situation, I will tend to "over" talk to God. Yes, we need to pray and talk to God, but in the middle of talking to Him, I can hear the Holy Spirit whisper so many times...."Shhhhhhhhh!"

It is so important to use our voice and speak, especially in prayer. It is so important to speak scripture over our lives and the lives of others...to be bold and courageous in the Lord and pick up the Sword of the Spirit! These are all excellent disciplines for believers, especially if you tend to be on the quiet side. But what if you are on the other end and need to turn the volume down? Sure, it can be easy to sing a praise song and REJOICE with music. But how do we REJOICE in the silence? And why is this discipline important too?

Have you ever stopped for maybe ten to twenty seconds and just listened to the thoughts that run through your mind? I tested this out one morning while having coffee on the porch. Also, I had my bible in hand, ready to read and pray. My quick thoughts in just 20 seconds:

"I need to check Instagram"

"What do I want for breakfast?"

"I need to exercise today"

"I need to text ____ to check on her"
"Why does that squirrel keep getting in my bird feeder?"
"I have GOT to vacuum today."
"I need to reheat my coffee."

If your mind is like mine (hoping I'm not the only one) it can be so hard to quiet down thoughts. Have you ever watched a news channel when they show updates on the stock market exchange and those scrolls of numbers and abbreviations go across the screen? That's what my mind seems like at times…lots of info, but most of it irrelevant.

Irrelevant thoughts are one thing, but our mind can also be full of frustrating, worrisome and fearful thoughts making our thoughts feel "LOUD!" Worry, doubt, fear, etc. are coming at our mind like missiles! Those times when the mind is so bombarded with "what ifs," it's hard to hear the voice of God. If God had installed a switch in my mind to turn off these kind of thoughts, I would probably use it frequently.

So how do we REJOICE and get quiet? It's an amazing discipline, and one we have to practice often in order for our mind, our time and our obedience to God to be fruitful and effective…and to keep our focus on how big God is. Let me help you, as I help me! Deal?

First, from a practical point of view, in order to get quiet with God, we sometimes have to change our position. My body, my whole self, has to be repositioned to refocus my thoughts. I have to sometimes literally get up from my sofa or chair, or stop pacing around the house, and drop to my knees in surrender. It's amazing how this works. My mind immediately slows down when my body bows to Jesus. My flesh quiets down and the devil backs off because he knows I'm in prayer mode. He sees my posture! My body goes low, but my spirit rises up!!

> *"Be still, and know that I am God!"*
> PSALM 46:10

Simple, yet this is a very powerful verse. The Hebrew word used for "be still" is a very visual word. It means to "sink down or low, to drop and relax." When we get on our knees or sometimes flat on our stomach and face down before God, we are "sinking low." It's a posture where you "let go and abandon." Visualize this, when you physically sink low before God, you also spiritually drop, abandon, and let go of everything. Weightless in His arms. Sinking low also magnifies that yes, He IS God. Now that's a quiet place to be and it also frees you up to REJOICE in serving a God that can shoulder EVERYTHING!

In Psalm 37:7-8, we can get really great instructions on being still,

> *"Be still in the presence of the Lord, and wait patiently for him to act. Don't worry about evil*

people who prosper or fret about their wicked schemes. Stop being angry! Turn from your rage! Do not lose your temper—it only leads to harm."

PSALM 37:7-8

What is interesting about the Hebrew word used for "be still" in this scripture means to "grow dumb in silence." Let's be real for a minute. When we OVER think an issue with worry and fear, or become overly obsessed with circumstances, we in essence are saying we are smarter than God or are having trust issues. Do you ever play over and over to God what is going on in your life? Do you ever tell Him what He needs to do to correct the matter? Do you ever just plain forget that He is God?

There are times we need to drop down, and totally focus our thoughts on Him to realize He sees all, knows all, and IS all! If I don't do the "be still in the presence of the Lord and wait patiently" part, then I can't do the other part of this verse. When I bow before the Lord in quiet and silence and realize how big He is, then I'm in a great position to cast my cares, release and resist anger, and turn the matter over to Him. I also position myself to patiently wait on Him. Picture completely leaning up against Jesus...the kind of leaning where your body is abandoned to Him...no props. That's trust...it's also a posture of rest.

I understand it's a challenge when life can be LOUD

and stormy. I have had those times throughout my life. Remember the story of the disciples and the storm? In Mark 4:37-41, Jesus and the disciples are in the Sea of Galilee heading for Gerasenes. The Sea of Galilee is more like a large lake, so this storm was not typical and it wasn't just blowing a little wind. This storm was like a hurricane building up… in a lake! Jesus' destination is to free a man from demons (Mark 5). Yes, there's a demon-possessed man living in the cemetery and he has affected a whole community. Do you believe unexpected "storms" can discourage us or side-track us from the Lord's work or from helping others? One thing is for sure, unexpected storms may bother us, but they don't shake Jesus one bit!

As Jesus continues to rest in the boat while it is tossed about, the disciples are in total fear.

> *"When Jesus woke up, he rebuked the wind and said to the waves, "Silence! Be still!" Suddenly the wind stopped, and there was a great calm."*
>
> MARK 4:39

They wake him up and he responds to the storm, "QUIET!" The water becomes slick as glass and the disciples witness yet another miracle to confirm Jesus is in charge. The imagery of this "Be still" is Jesus taking the storm in his grip and muzzling it! I picture a big, bad, ferocious dog barking and growling with teeth exposed and foaming at the mouth. But when you muzzle that dog, all of its intimidation and power is halted! Wow! That's power!

I also love Jesus' response to the disciples,

> "Why are you afraid? Do you still have no faith?"
> MARK 4:40

Part of me wants to say, "Hey Jesus, it was a storm! Of course they were afraid." But Jesus expects more from them; after all, they have already seen and experienced many miracles. He expected them to stay God-focused and stop being distracted or impressed with evil and outside influences. Do you think He says that to us too depending on our experiences with Him?

Never doubt, Jesus IS in charge. This world's system may be run by evil, but God is Almighty and He is GOOD. In the days we are in now, hearing from God is very important. Not only hearing, but then being obedient to His direction and allowing Him to show us how to pray. There is so much noise in the world. Social Media dominates, and while it can be used for good, it can also be addicting. I admit, grabbing my phone requires no thought or planning...I can just mindlessly scroll Instagram, or YouTube and before I know it an hour can pass by. In the days ahead, more discipline is required in order for us to be prepared. This is not a statement of fear, but an alertness that we need to be the most effective Christ followers in our witness, thinking, actions and prayer life. I'm "preaching to the choir" when I say, it's time to get in shape for Jesus!

Hebrews 12:1-2 says,

> *"Therefore, since we are surrounded by such a huge crowd of witnesses to the life of faith, let us strip off every weight that slows us down, especially that sin that so easily trips us up. And let us run with endurance the race God has set before us. We do this by keeping our eyes on Jesus, the champion who initiates and perfects our faith."*
>
> HEBREWS 12:1-2

In order to keep our eyes on Jesus and run the race before us, we have to be aware of our distractions. This includes physical, mental and emotional distractions. All of these can keep us weighed down. Be still! Become weightless in Him. Shhhhhhh! It's time for Jesus to be LOUD in our lives!

Let's practice being still…..

- First, move your body from that comfy sofa or chair, and kneel or lay flat before the Lord, if you are physically able.
- With no prayer agenda or petition, tell the Lord you would like to get quiet before Him and by faith be in

His Presence.
- Then, by faith, tell the Lord you would like to release your thoughts, fears and distractions to Him…then choose to lay them down, as if you were abandoning them at His feet.
- Next, invite the Holy Spirit to speak, minister, prompt scripture, or do whatever He would like to do.
- Relax, sink down in Him. Enjoy the Silence and Stillness of an Awesome God.
- Shhhhhhh…The quiet sound of Rejoicing

SECTION FIVE

Would You Be Willing To Realign?

Before we begin this section, I just want to say that I was almost finished with this book WITHOUT this section. I loved the simplicity of 5 sections and 30 chapters. I liked the flow of it and I was very pleased with all I had shared, both personally and from scripture. I liked knowing that I was only a few paragraphs away from wrapping up and handing off to my friend to typeset and put it into book form. I liked the feeling of knowing my part was about finished! Yet for some reason those last few paragraphs in the final chapter were not flowing. Something was missing and I wasn't sure why I felt stalled. Then I realized there is more to the "Would

You Be Willing?" part that is very important. It's the part I personally deal with on a frequent basis. Maybe it is a part you deal with too?

The only way I know to write this section is to share MY struggles and what the Lord has taught me. It's those times when I either strayed from my closeness with God or times when I do things my way and let my fleshly nature be in charge. And when that happens, I realize I've either been walking in sin, or maybe I've just neglected time with God. Either way, I do what I call...REALIGNMENT!

Has your car ever suddenly started veering to the right or left, and it takes more effort to keep it centered? When that happens, you have to be more aware of steering the car. When you're out of alignment, the steering wheel can even vibrate, indicating there's a problem. You may think you're driving straight, but the car is actually driving crooked! When this happens, the tires track unevenly, which puts pressure on the tires and they push against each other. Friction occurs and you have more resistance from driving on the road...as opposed to having a smooth drive! No matter how straight you try to drive, there is a force pulling against you! If this isn't addressed, you could end up spending a lot of money to fix the problem, not to mention increasing the dangers in driving...for you and for others on the road!

I may not know a lot about cars, but I know when I need to take my car in for realignment. Driving a car out of alignment is about as annoying as choosing that ONE cart at the grocery store that needs realignment!!! Those close grocery aisles become an obstacle course as you fight that cart to keep it from hitting the shelves or another buggy. That misaligned buggy can steal your joy quicker that anything!!

Let's think of theses analogies in terms of our spiritual life. Have there been times you felt out of alignment with God? Where you feel the vibration of conviction in your heart? Instead of peace and contentment, your spiritual drive feels bumpy and aggravating? Since I can't hear your stories, I'll share a few of mine!! Here goes being transparent! Spiritual realignment isn't always easy, but when we yield to God and realign walking, listening, and being obedient to Him, boy does the spiritual path become smoother!!

CHAPTER TWENTY FIVE

Pushing Off Or Pulling Up!

One time I had a loving family member bring to my attention that I was gossiping about someone I had ministered to. I was shocked, because I didn't believe I was gossiping at all....I was simply sharing about our ministry time, and how I had spiritually advised this person and prayed. I did not mention the personal's name or details, just more a general observation. This family member pointed out that I talked too much about the ministry situation and biblically, that was gossip. This allegation hurt my feelings and frankly, embarrassed me a little. It got me thinking, "would I have shared the information if that person were here?"

Several months later I was a part of an art show and over the weekend of sharing my artwork, meeting new people and artists, I found myself in a conversation I shouldn't have been in. Although I was chatting with a fellow artist, I disclosed personal disappointment I had toward a retail business. After the weekend was over I was reflecting on the wonderful people I met and the great time I had….yet, in the midst of praising God and thanking Him for His goodness for a productive weekend….He halted my praise and brought conviction on my heart. He took me to that unnecessary discussion, and showed me that I was gossiping.

I quickly repented and received His forgiveness. But what also happened was I remembered what my family member said. At that point, I didn't just want to repent and ask forgiveness, then move on. I wanted to understand the "whys" of gossiping and what happens spiritually. I wanted to **REALIGN** back with God, but I wanted scriptural understanding. Honestly, for spiritual principles to stick with me, I have to have more than just conviction. It's like in a relationship. For example, I can unknowingly hurt my daughter's feelings and follow up with "I'm sorry," but if she explains to me "why" she was hurt, then I'm less likely to do it again. How much more in a relationship with God do we need to understand the "whys?" First, let's look at some scriptures related to gossip:

"Who may worship in your sanctuary, Lord? Who may enter your presence on your holy hill? Those who lead blameless lives and do what is right, speaking the truth from sincere hearts. Those who refuse to gossip or harm their neighbors or speak evil of their friends."

PSALM 5:1-3

"A gossip goes around telling secrets, but those who are trustworthy can keep a confidence."

PROVERBS 11:13

"Wrongdoers eagerly listen to gossip; liars pay close attention to slander."

PROVERBS 17:4

"A gossip goes around telling secrets, so don't hang around with chatterers."

PROVERBS 20:19

*"Their lives became full of every kind of wickedness, sin, greed, hate, envy, murder, quarreling,

> *deception, malicious behavior, and gossip."*
>
> ROMANS 1:29

> *"For I am afraid that when I come I won't like what I find, and you won't like my response. I am afraid that I will find quarreling, jealousy, anger, selfishness, slander, gossip, arrogance, and disorderly behavior."*
>
> 2 CORINTHIANS 12:20

This is just a handful of scriptures. There are many more, especially ones using the word slander, which is a synonym to the word gossip. At the end of this chapter I'll note more scripture references you can check out on your own. It's very obvious that God hates gossip. So much so that it is combined with other evil words like murder, wickedness, jealousy, etc. Therefore, this word should not be taken lightly. We need to take the effects of gossip seriously and stay far away from it!

In studying this word, I came across scripture passages that were a game changer: 1 Timothy 1:5-6, 1 Timothy 1:19 and 1 Timothy 3:11. It is worth reading the book of 1 Timothy, because it gives Christians strict guidelines on a variety of church topics, like worship, false teachings, church leadership and responsibilities of the church people. Yet as I was searching a more in-depth study for gossip, this is where my eyes were opened.

> "The purpose of my instruction is that all believers would be filled with love that comes from <u>a pure heart, a clear conscience, and genuine faith</u>! But some people have missed this whole point. They have turned away from these things and spend their time in <u>meaningless discussions</u>."
>
> 1 TIMOTHY 1:5-6

> "**<u>Cling</u>** to your faith in Christ, and <u>keep your conscience clear</u>. For some people have **deliberately violated** <u>their conscience</u>; as a result their faith has been shipwrecked."
>
> 1 TIMOTHY 1:19

> "In the same way, their wives must be respected and <u>must not slander others</u>. They <u>must exercise self-control and be faithful in everything they do</u>."
>
> 1 TIMOTHY 3:11

Now, before it enters anyone's mind, we will NOT be discussing church leadership or women in the church. We WILL take a look at God's expectation for the believer and the character we should have because we belong to Him.

In Paul's letter to Timothy, he warns Timothy that false teachings will creep into the church. Theses teachings are not only a bunch of myths, but real time-wasters that will affect the hearts of the people. He says that listening and being in meaningless discussions will actually affect our faith. He shares that the goal for ALL believers is to walk in love which comes from <u>a pure heart,</u> <u>a clear conscience</u> and <u>genuine faith</u>.

So if my love for people is not lining up with these three points, then there's a tendency to get into meaningless discussions. Why? Because I have turned from walking in these specific characteristics. These three areas will not automatically fall on a person, but they have to be practiced and they have to be intentional. By getting into a meaningless discussion at the art show, I was not walking in love. I was walking in opinions, pride, and frankly, I just wanted to talk and impress the listener. If I had been walking in love, I would have been more concerned about protecting "a pure heart and clear conscience." Yet I stepped out of my faith, and totally stepped into my flesh. My mouth took control, while my conscience screamed "Stop!"

Come on, if we are a follower of Jesus and we spend time in the Word of God, we KNOW when we have crossed the line. It's like a war goes off inside ourselves…we're making our flesh feel really good and excited, while our heart is feeling pierced and guilty. And because I was not "walking by faith in Christ," I did what verse 6 said, "<u>Violated my conscience and shipwrecked my faith</u>." Wow! Sounds a little strong, doesn't it. I mean after all, I was just talking about a factual experience and a real perspective. Right? Then why didn't I feel peaceful about it? Let's take a closer look at verse 19:

> "<u>Cling to your faith in Christ</u>, and keep your conscience clear. For some people have deliberately violated their conscience."
>
> 1 TIMOTHY 3:19

To "cling" in the original Greek language is "to hold one's self to." To hold myself to what? To FAITH in Christ! It is my responsibility to walk in faith by holding tightly to Jesus, otherwise I can easily violate my conscience by doing something like gossip! I am the one who chooses to gossip. I am the one who chooses to deliberately violate my conscience. The Greek visual here means to "thrust away or push away." That's not passive, but some strong decisions I make when I choose to gossip, slander or talk negative about someone.

In fact, the pull of gossip is so strong that the Word says I have to CLING to Jesus in order to stay away from it! But the reward for clinging is a pure heart and clear conscience. I can sleep better at night with that, can't you?

Believe it or not, this was just the easy lesson about the consequences of gossiping. Now let's look at 1 Timothy 3:11,

> "In the same way, their wives must be respected and

> *must not slander others. They must exercise self-control and be faithful in everything they do."*
>
> 1 TIMOTHY 3:11

This raises the bar!!! Before this verse, Paul is explaining some of the traits, characteristics and guidelines for church elders and deacons. Not just anyone could take on these roles in the church...there was a standard. Some may think, "yeah, but we all make mistakes and nobody's perfect."

Question: If you owned a business, wouldn't you hire people who represented you in a positive way? Wouldn't you expect a certain standard of ethics, moral behaviors, professionalism, authenticity, etc? After all, those employees represent YOU! So why should running a church be any different? We are Christ Followers following AND representing God! Moving on...

So Paul goes from the job description of the elders and deacons, to the expectation of their wives! As a Christian married woman, I totally get this. Because I'm in covenant with my husband, the way I act, think and feel doesn't just effect me, but it effects him too! And vice versa! We can either complement each other in representing Christ, or butt heads in conflict!

Paul spends a few paragraphs talking about the requirements for the elders and deacons, but I find it interesting that he really only brings out one main point when talking about how their wives should act! He says they "must not slander!" Paul could have said, "wives should be good cooks, strong in hospitality, have hearts for the children, have delightful personalities"....but no, Paul lets us know that with the women in that church, there was an issue with gossip...that's why he brought it up and made a deliberate point.

Ladies, before we get all bristled up and turn our backs on Paul, let's get honest with ourselves as women. I clearly remember from the time I was in elementary school all the way through college sorority....GIRLS GOSSIP! We compare, size up, tear down and destroy our own! I believe gossip is one of the primary things that tears down and divides women. Why do we do that? This isn't hard...IT'S SIN! Our carnal nature is wired that way! That's why we MUST respect people and choose NOT to slander others.

What I love about Paul is he's not picking on women, but using his gift of boldness to help them. He also had an amazing gift of being able to take the weaknesses of a church and bring correction for the purpose of strengthening the people as a whole. His writings are still doing that today!

So out of curiosity, I decided to dig deep and see what the Greek word for "gossip" is. Are you ready? Seriously, are you ready? It was an eye-opener for me and made me realize it is serious business and why God hates it. OK, here goes...

The Greek word for gossip/slander is "Diabolos"....an

adjective where we get the word Diabolical!!!! Here's the full Greek meaning:

"Prone to slander; slanderous; accusing falsely; a calumniator; opposing God; to act the part of the devil or to side with him"

My first thought when I read this was movies where the villain is referred to as "diabolical." That character who thinks up evil in order to oppose good! What? Surely gossip isn't that strong….is it?

The verb meaning in the Greek is "diaballo" which means "to throw over or across, to send over to slander, accuse or deframe (like tearing down piece by piece)" Breaking down this word even further:

"dia" – preposition – accusative division into two or more parts

"ballo" – to throw or let go of a thing without caring where it falls

I hope by now you're getting a visual of this. Gossiping or slander is like physically taking that person over to say, the edge of a cliff, and pushing them off…without caring where they land! It's the visual of also taking something that should be whole and deliberately ripping it into parts! Oh friends, this isn't who I am and I doubt it's who you are either! We are called to the ministry of oneness in the Body of Christ! We are called to save, rescue and help others….not push people off cliffs!

As verse 3:11 says, I MUST NOT gossip, because first, it sides me with the devil, instead of with God. Secondly, in order to not gossip (which remember, my flesh wants to because it opposes the Spirit), I have to do the rest of verse 11...EXERCISE SELF-CONTROL AND BE FAITHFUL. We have to have the MUST part, which is choosing obedience to God.

Exercising self-control means it's something we have to practice and ask the Holy Spirit to help us with. It's one of the fruit of the Spirit (Galatians 5:22-23), so I need the Holy Spirit's empowerment, which I have total access to as a believer. Self-control is not just to keep me out of trouble, it's a godly character trait. It has to be practiced or exercised, which also means, it's not something that comes naturally, but supernaturally through obedience to God's ways! Discipline and obedience to the Lord will fight and win against gossip and slander!

So let's use my life example to bring this all together. By the way, this was a little painful to share, but I want to be transparent, so hopefully we all can be strengthened. When I was talking negatively in my discussion at the art show, I was tearing down those people and siding with Satan. Plus my discussion was to an unbeliever! AND the people I was talking about were BELIEVERS. I'll never forget getting in the car that night and the Spirit of the Lord said loud and clear, "So let's see, you gossiped to an unbeliever about sisters in

Christ...was that a good witness?" I knew then I had to not only repent, but get delivered, reclaim and start walking in self-control and obedience.

The territory of gossip is very dark and diabolical. The territory of self-control and kindness is full of light. Not a hard choice, but it requires the help of the Holy Spirit and exercising that spiritual muscle. I need His help to give lots of grace and to love at all times. I need His help to cover other's flaws with love; instead of pointing out what I think are their flaws. After all, I certainly hope I'm treated that way by others, don't you? Oh how the principle of sowing and reaping goes in both directions....positive OR negative!

As a Christ follower, we are called to a higher standard. Paul explains this to young Timothy in Chapter 4, verse 12...

> *"Be an example to all believers in what you say, in the way you live, in your love, your faith, and your purity."*
>
> 1 TIMOTHY 4:12

- What I say….Matters
- The way I live….Matters
- The way I love others…Matters
- My faith in Christ….Matters
- Walking in purity…Matters

Am I still tempted at times to speak negatively about someone? Sure! Especially if that person has hurt me or I see

Pushing Off Or Pulling Up

them hurting others! My flesh wants to speak against them, because the reasoning is they deserve it! Then I get the visual and God saying, "Do you want to be obedient and pray for them, or push them off a cliff?" I have to choose to align myself with God. Every single time. Realign.

After the Lord convicted me and taught me the seriousness of gossip, not only did I repent, but in prayer I pictured myself going to the bottom of the cliff and helping them up and dusting them off. I pictured myself saying how sorry I was. Then I intentionally spoke out loud blessings over the individuals. Peace came and a lesson was learned.

In this whole visual lesson, I also realized that it's more productive as a believer to help people who slander themselves. We all know those who curse or speak negatively over their lives, or over their family's lives. We can help others by "pulling them from the edge of the cliff" by praying for them and when given the opportunity, speak positive, life-giving words over them!

Would you be willing to realign with the Lord in the area of our words towards others?

Let's pray...

"Heavenly Father, forgive me and deliver me from the spirit of gossip and slander. I want to realign my mouth with You, and be more aware of the weight of my words. Lord, my desire is to speak words of life and blessings,

especially over the Body of Christ. Help me, Holy Spirit, to exercise self-control and not let my flesh vent negative words. I would much rather walk in Your peace, than try to be right in a conversation. Help me pray for others who have brought pain or hurt to me and to put those situations in Your hands. Lord, I desire for my words to represent You. You continuously treat me with kindness, patience and love....help me to treat others the same. In Jesus' Name... Amen!"

Other Realignment Scriptures:

- Leviticus 19:16
- Psalm 101:5
- Proverbs 16:28
- Proverbs 26:20
- Proverbs 30:10
- Jeremiah 6:28
- Ephesians 4:31
- Colossians 3:8
- Titus 3:1-2
- James 4:11
- 1 Peter 2:1

CHAPTER TWENTY SIX

He Works In The Waiting

Have you ever prayed for God to move in a situation, and it seems like He is either not listening or He is on vacation? Sure, you know you may have to wait for a period of time before you see the breakthrough, but what happens when the answer delays....REALLY delays. When days turn into weeks and weeks turn into years! And you feel like you've done your part, like praying, agreement prayer with friends, positive confession, rebuking the enemy, and quoting the scriptures. You read books, listened to tapes, podcasts and cranked up the praise music. You've even turned it on yourself and thought, "Lord, am I in sin and that's why You are delaying?" You don't get a reply, so you go ahead and try to think of any sins you may not have repented of just in case. Then you decide, maybe, He wants YOU to do something, which would speed up the process of this miracle. So you take matters in your own hands, because those ideas popping in your head seem brilliant...until you act on them. Then in a matter of seconds it seems you've taken 10 steps backwards, instead of 2 steps forward! You are so discouraged that doubt creeps in, and you wonder if He even cares about you. Or you wonder if He is even real. You go from praying all of the time, to numbness to prayer. In the confusion of trying to figure out the whole thing, you even lose sight of your purpose. Then the saddest feeling of all becomes a heavy weight on your mind and heart when you conclude, "Can I trust You, God?"

Well, that was a depressing paragraph, wasn't it!?! If you haven't experienced all of these feelings, I bet you've experienced a few of them. As Christ followers, we all have petitions and prayer requests to God. After all, He tells us to pray about everything! Jesus said,

> *"Ask anything in my name, and I will do it!"*
> JOHN 14:13-14

So why does it seem like at times He's not doing anything? My answer is...I don't know. But here's what I do know.

The longer I wait for my prayers to be answered, the more Mary Jo changes...and I'm not talking good changes! Waiting on God produces a whole host of behaviors in me, which frankly, are not flattering at all! Behaviors that DO NOT reflect Christ in me! I can become **pitiful, anxious, negative, impatient,** and **complaining**. In other words, I will PANIC!!! (See what I did with those letters there?) And when I panic, I am the polar opposite of trusting God. I have also come to the point where I have become so consumed with whatever it is I'm believing God for, that it can be all I think about, pray about, and talk about. At that point friends, not only have I stopped trusting God, but I have made that thing an idol!! Therefore, I have to REALIGN.

First, I do have to recognize that my behavior is a problem. Oh sure, we think that we have every right at times to walk in PANIC, especially when we've believed for a long time. It's like we're wearing this prayer badge we think we've earned. We've checked off all the spiritual requirements to earn the badge with all of the confessions, rebuking, quoting scripture, and praise music. Not to mention the tears, begging and pleading. Oh, I've been there. During a season of caregiving for my dad, I became so tired, frustrated and pitiful, that I did the unthinkable. I was so mad at God's performance... I ripped up my Jesus Calling devotional! (I can hear you gasping!!!) January thru December was torn and tossed all over the place. Seeing those pages that once had been a source of strength, were now disrespected papers on the carpet. Yet, as soon as my emotions died down and I saw the damage, I wept. What had I done? I destroyed the very thing I cherished. As I gathered the pages one by one, and put them in order, I realized I had to realign with God. I also had to ask the question, "If circumstances never change, can I still love, worship and follow God? Can I have peace and joy in the midst of disappointment? Can I trust God and lay down this prayer I've been consumed with?" I also had to ask a very sobering question, "Do I like myself like this?" Of course, the answer was 100%...NO!

God's timeframe is not like ours. He is never shocked or comes unglued with our circumstances. He is never caught off guard, nor is He without a plan. He sees all things, knows all things and perfects those things He's concerned with… including ME! When I'm a little bent out of shape with God's performance, I have to remember that He is the Potter and I am the clay! God didn't create me for me…He created me for Him. He desires me to know who I am IN HIM. If my God, through His son, Jesus, laid down His life for me, then no matter how I feel at the time, TRUTH says GOD LOVES ME. And if He loves me, I can trust Him. Again, in the waiting the prayer has to be, "Lord, until my prayer is answered… change me."

Also, the older I get, if I can just wrap myself in His peace, then I know I'm OK. If I expand my thinking and realize I have a relationship with the King of Kings and Lord of Lords, then all will be fine. Sometimes God's delays are working for good, even though it just doesn't seem that way in the situation. Sometimes He will answer the prayers His way, not always exactly how we prayed or believed for the outcome. Also, we have to make sure the way we approach Him isn't just to get a certain outcome, but to release and let go of our way. We have to trust that His way is the best way and He IS a good God. I base how things are going by how I feel and how outward things are affecting my life. He desires for me to mature and look more like Him.

If I realign away from my PANIC, and focus back on Him and what a godly, mature behavior should look like, then my mind, my thoughts and my body will calm down...and yes, wait a little longer. When Paul wrote letters to various churches, he always pointed out things that were more important during our short time on earth. Let's see what he says:

> *"Dear brothers and sisters, I close my letter with these last words: Be joyful. Grow to maturity. Encourage each other. Live in harmony and peace. THEN the God of love and peace will be with you."*
>
> 2 CORINTHIANS 13:11

> *"What counts is whether we have been transformed into a new creation. May God's peace and mercy be upon all who live by this principle; they are the new people of God."*
>
> GALATIANS 6:15-16

> *"For I want you to understand what really matters, so that you may live pure and blameless lives until the day of Christ's return. May you always be filled with the fruit of your salvation – the righteous character produced in your life by Jesus Christ – for this will bring much glory and praise to God."*
>
> PHILIPPIANS 1:10-11

Instead of MY spiritual checklist focusing on MY prayers, how about a new checklist? One that focuses on the things Paul said were MOST important:

- Choose to be joyful
- Grow up
- Encourage other people
- Choose to be a peaceful person
- Desire to be transformed daily in His image
- Live for Jesus and bear fruit in my character
- Glorify and Praise God

And by the way, I don't have to work on my list by myself...the Holy Spirit is helping me! Now realignment puts me where I need to be...Trusting God.

"Lord, sometimes life is exhausting and I struggle, doubting that You are listening to my prayers. Yet I will proclaim, "I Trust You." As I go through valleys, let godly character, maturity, and deeper trust in You develop in me. Help me, Holy Spirit, to quickly take PANIC behaviors and with Your strength, choose Christ-like behaviors. Even when my feelings aren't lining up, I am willing to choose Your ways. Help me stay humble before You with praise, thanksgiving and adoration. I trust Your timing. In Jesus' Name. AMEN"

CHAPTER TWENTY SEVEN

The Need For Peeps

I have always been a "people" person and God has blessed me over the years with some amazing friends. Friends who make me laugh, encourage me, pray for me, and love me so well. Yet I can tell as I get older I tend to pull back and like my alone time. That's not a bad thing, in fact, we need quiet moments just to relax, chill and refresh. Times of silence can be the sweetest sound ever!!!! This is a healthy quiet with a healthy mindset and a great thing to practice! But there is also unhealthy silence. Those times when we retreat in seclusion and isolate ourselves from others, because we are thinking negatively or depressed. What is our mindset during this kind of silence?

For years my husband has prayed a certain way when he prays in a group setting. It goes something like this, *"Lord, Your Word teaches us that everything is about relationships, and the importance of relationships. Thank you that we can be in relationship with these friends and family"*...and so on and so forth. For a while I'd think, "come on, switch up it a bit!" Lord, help me!! What he was confessing was the truth! We have to have relationships! One of the most effective tactics of Satan is if he can successfully isolate the believer! We were never meant to be islands and handle life's difficulties alone. We were meant to connect!!!

The most important relationship we will ever have is a relationship with God through Jesus. All the way back in the Old Testament, God makes it crystal clear that He wants a relationship with man and for man to see that relationship as priority. In Exodus 34:14 relating to one of the Ten Commandments,

> *"You must worship no other gods, for the Lord, whose very name is Jealous, is a God who is jealous about relationship with you."*
>
> EXODUS 34:14

Of course, this is not a weird, selfish, or insecure kind of jealous, but a jealous so powerful and passionate that He never wants to be apart from us. A love so strong that for us to be pulled away from Him is painful and hurtful to Him. A jealous love that laid down His life for us...wow, that's love! And it's a relationship so hard to understand with our human mind.

I love when Paul describes this love relationship in Ephesians 3:19 when he says,

> "May you experience the love of Christ, though it is too great to understand fully."
>
> EPHESIANS 3:19

We just can't completely wrap our mind or heart around His kind of love! And out of this great love, He does desire us to be in relationship with each other. Remember, a healthy, jealous love always encourages relationships that connect with others, while unhealthy, jealous love isolates and discourages relationships. This isn't a hard principle... relationship connects, while isolation pulls apart. If we are not clear on these meanings and aware of our mindset, then we may need some realignment. Let's look a little deeper into isolation and why it's a path to avoid.

In the dictionary the word isolate means:

"Cause to be and remain alone or apart from others"

"Separate, detach, cut off, shut away or keep in solitude"

Another definition I thought was interesting was, "one

who socially isolates becomes careless of their own welfare." Wow! When the enemy says in our head, *"Nobody will understand, so you shouldn't share,"* or *"You are better off alone, because you can't trust people,"* well, that's a sure sign that you NEED relationships for the sake of your welfare! Ironically, there is a time to isolate and a time to share…a time to seclude and stay silent and a time to testify and share. Mindset is key.

Let's look at "relationship and isolation" all in the same story! In Luke, chapter 1 we meet a priest, Zechariah and his wife, Elizabeth. This couple was up in years and walked with God all of their lives, yet never had the blessing of children, because Elizabeth was barren. Zechariah was in a priestly lineage, and performed his duties in the temple (read Luke 1:8-10). While on duty, an angel appeared to him and delivered the overwhelming news that he and Elizabeth were going to be parents! And this was not just any child, but one prophesied about in the Old Testament…John the Baptist! Zechariah was so shocked that he reminds the angel that he must have the wrong guy, because he and his bride were OLD! The angel, Gabriel, shut down and shut up all the doubt…literally! Zechariah remained mute until John was born! After his temple service ended, he returned home and sure enough, Elizabeth was pregnant!!!

Now let's look at verse 1:24,

"Soon afterward his wife, Elizabeth, became pregnant

and went into seclusion for five months."

LUKE 1:24

Oh no! Five months of seclusion is not healthy right? Well, let's look at the next verse to see Elizabeth's mindset. Verse 25 says,

"How kind the Lord is!" she exclaimed. "He has taken away my disgrace of having no children."

LUKE 1:24

Elizabeth was praising God and secluded herself with a heart and mind of rejoicing! Whether it was a cultural thing, or just the sheer joy of a miracle, she knew this was not the time to chat with girlfriends, but to spend time with God and her husband and prepare for what was coming! She wanted to take great care of what and who God had entrusted to her. Too much talk would have totally diluted this holy, intimate time and I believe Elizabeth knew it!

Healthy alone time with God can be a powerful time! Elizabeth knew that too much talk of this pregnancy could have caused this couple to fear, doubt or reject this miracle. They didn't need to get opinions, confirmations, or a prayer chain started. They needed to wait on God and get direction from Him. Elizabeth knew she wouldn't remain in isolation… just a temporary sabbatical.

Meanwhile, her young cousin, Mary, received a visit from the angel too! We know the story of this young, virgin girl who says "yes" to become pregnant with God's child. We know Mary said yes to the assignment, but let's look at her mindset. Verse 29 says,

> *"Confused and disturbed, Mary tried to think what the angel could mean."*
>
> LUKE 1:29

I'm thinking that's an understandable reaction! Gabriel immediately tells her not to be afraid, which logically would mean, she was afraid. Mary innocently asked, "How is this going to happen?" Gabriel proceeds to explain who this baby will become and how it will happen. That's a lot of information to take in, so Gabriel switches gears and shares some more wonderful news....Elizabeth is pregnant too! Why is that great news?

If I had been Mary, my mind would have been spinning while Gabriel is giving all of the heavenly details of something so unbelievable that it would be hard to fathom. I would definitely be confused and disturbed for sure! But hearing that my elderly cousin was pregnant with a miracle baby! Now I'd have someone to relate to! Mary NEEDED relationship! She received heavy news and she needed wisdom, guidance and the understanding of an older woman.

Mary decided to make about a three day journey to Elizabeth's house. And God does the sweetest thing!!! I love how God is so understanding! Before Mary could deliver her unbelievable news to her elderly cousin, Elizabeth, filled with the Holy Spirit, shouts, "You are blessed and pregnant with God's child!!!"

OK that's not exactly what she says, but that sums it up! Can't you just see the relief on Mary's face! These two godly women spent time encouraging, praying and relating to each other.

I'd like to share one more thing about relationships and encouraging one another. Years ago I was sitting in my doctor's office having post discussion after my annual physical examination. I had started a new job and was feeling very tired and was low on physical and mental energy. My doctor asked me some logical questions like, "How are your eating habits?" "How are your sleeping habits?" "Are you exercising?" Then he asked a question that I wasn't expecting... "Are you having girlfriend time?"

What? Girlfriend time? Why would that have anything to do with my physical body?

He told me that it was a scientific fact that women need POSITIVE fellowship time with other women. He said when women encourage, spend quality time and support one another; it affects them in a positive way physically, as it does socially, emotionally and mentally. He recommended I call up one of my sisters in Christ and schedule coffee time! Now that's an awesome prescription!

Having Christian girlfriends is so important! I have some amazing ones! They sharpen me spiritually and point me to Jesus! They pray for me and correct me when I need it! The best girlfriends are the ones who inspire and empower you and vice versa. We need each other on this journey! It matters!

If you need time alone, by all means, take it!! Make sure your mindset is healthy and you're focused on God. But if you are feeling depressed, pitiful, tired or spiritually dry, then isolation is dangerous. There's nothing like sharing with a trusted friend who will listen and pray. So grab that coffee and connect! We need people!! We need each other!! Relationship with others brings fresh perspective, keeps us moving forward and most of all; it can REALIGN a wrong mindset!

"Heavenly Father, thank you it was Your idea to create relationships. How humbling it is to know that You want an intimate relationship with me. As I draw near to You, You draw near to me! Increase desire in me to grow in relationship with You and make it a priority. Lord, help me to be aware of healthy and unhealthy mindsets. When I need a friend, I trust you to show me who to call. When I need to have godly silent time, speak to my heart and fill me up! Keep me from being a island and help me discern

any attacks on my mind. Also, help me be aware when someone needs me to speak encouraging words to them or share my testimony. In Jesus' Name, AMEN."

"As iron sharpens iron, so a friend sharpens a friend."

PROVERBS 27:17

CHAPTER TWENTY EIGHT

What Did You Say?...
Sorry, I Was Distracted

Remember my friend Lisa from the introduction? When I would go over to her house in high school, sometimes we would watch TV. During a show she would try to talk to me, but I was so absorbed in the episode I wouldn't hear her. She would say, "Mary, stop watching TV and listen!" I hate to admit it, but if the television was on, I was totally distracted! Remember, I told you at the beginning of this section that I was sharing my realignment stories...well, this is a one of them I'm working on! Television, YouTube and social media can totally distract me!

There are a handful of movies that I love! If, by chance,

one of them is on as I click through the channels...I HAVE to watch it! It can be at the beginning of the movie, the middle, or toward the end...doesn't matter. Although I've seen it a million times...I see it through until the credits roll!

Here's another weakness I have. It's not chocolate or potato chips, although I hardly ever turn down either. This may sound strange, but I LOVE watching makeover shows! There's just something about seeing a woman radiant with joy when she sees herself with a new hairstyle, makeup, and clothes. I use to always watch *What Not To Wear* season after season. Now my favorite is Hoda and Kathie Lee's *Ambush Makeover*. Sometimes when it's 10:00pm and I'm not sleepy, I'll pull up YouTube and watch a few episodes. Here's the problem...you can't just watch a few. It's like trying to eat that one chip! So I watch and watch and before I know it, its 1:00am! The next morning I soon realize my body needed the three hours of sleep that I spent watching YouTube. Binge-watching can easily get a hold of me!

Last one. As an artist and author, I have an Instagram, which helps me connect with clients, friends and other artists. It allows me to share pictures of my recent paintings, books and also personal pictures of my family and friends. It's positive and fun...but can also consume my time. So here's what can happen. I finish a painting I'm so proud of and I share on my Instagram. Then I check, and recheck... and recheck my post to see how many "likes" and comments

I received. It's like waiting on approval stickers! Yet, I have to make sure that the weight of my follower's responses or lack of responses doesn't outweigh God's approval or opinion of me! Checking that app can become very addictive. Your fingers can be in such a habit of clicking that you don't even realize it!

There's nothing evil about watching makeover shows, or staying up too late. Nothing sinful about watching old reruns or checking Instagram. Yet once that time is gone…it's gone. Each one of us has our own set of familiar distractions. Here is the definition of distraction:

"A thing that prevents someone from giving full attention to something else."

The "thing" doesn't have to be evil or sinful. Yet if that "thing" prevents me from time with God, prayer, quality time with family, friends, being productive at work etc, then it can go from the category of entertainment, to the category of a distraction. Everybody's distractions are different. Distractions come in all shapes and sizes. Listen, you will never see me distracted with video games…my hand/eye coordination can't do it! Oh, and if you love taking all day shopping trips…I'm probably not your shopping buddy. Unless you're buying!

We understand how distractions work in today's relationships. It's very common to see two people eating in a restaurant across from each other. They are having zero conversation and both are on their cell phones! I have been so guilty of this too! That device is so attached to us!

Here's another example I've had to confront…having information at my fingertips. Let's say I'm watching a movie and there's an actor who looks familiar. What do I do? Grab the phone and Google that person, then scroll to see all the movies they've been in. Because if I don't, it will be on my mind till I solve the mystery. In seconds we can even find the actor's height, weight and birthday too! Seriously! Is it good to always have information instantaneously? We can be so consumed with irrelevant information and all it does is take up "mind-room."

The most important, eternal, life-changing relationship we will ever have on this earth is a relationship with God through His Son Jesus Christ. Allowing those "things" to distract me from Him is not wise. It's sad that I can expect so much from God, yet not honor Him with my undivided attention. Good News!!! It's never too late to realign!

As I have prayed and asked the Lord to help me, here are some practical things He's shown me. My mind or my thoughts, can only handle so much mixture of information. If He created me to be in a holy relationship with him, then building a relationship with Him requires knowing Him through His Word and spending time or experiencing Him. So if I fill my thoughts with movies, social media, YouTube, and worldly stuff, then there is limited room for the God stuff.

It's like numbing my thinking with worthless information. Think of it like binge-eating. My body was designed by the Master to function best on fruits, veggies, lean meats and whole grains. Yet when I spend a day feasting and getting full on food with zero nutrition...processed sugars, fried foods, fatty foods etc...well, I feel horrible! Headache, bloating, indigestion, or heartburn attacks my body and I'm searching for the Advil and Pepsid! One brownie is fine, but a pan of brownies is out of balance! My body can't function on junk food, and my mind can't function on junk information. Just like too much junk food can open doors to physical problems, likewise, too much junk information can attack the mind too. And just like fruits and vegetables bring my body nutrition, God's Word brings my mind and life spiritual nutrition.

Our mind is like a recorder...what goes in stores as data. So when I waste too much mind power and become too preoccupied with other things, it becomes very difficult to pray, retain scripture, or hear the voice of the Holy Spirit. What goes in, does come out!

Isn't it funny how focusing on a two hour movie is effortless compared to focusing on scripture, prayer or communicating with God? Spiritually speaking, the devil doesn't care if I focus on that movie...but he certainly cares when I absorb the Word, take up my authority in prayer, and use my mouth to praise God! He'll take advantage of distracting me as much as possible. But I don't want to give the devil too much credit! My flesh and my spirit are opposed to each other. My fleshly, sinful nature has to be disciplined to focus on God. It has to be controlled and made obedient to Christ. I have to be willing to realign and decide what has eternal value and what is best for my body, soul and spirit. If I'm soaking up God, then the people I love and others benefit!

Let's not let the noise of the world distract us from the voice of God. If we ARE distracted, then let's repent and realign! Jesus talked about distraction when he was sharing the parable of the farmer scattering seed in Mark 4:1-20. In verse 18-19, Jesus says,

> *"The seed that fell among the thorns represents those who hear God's word, but all too quickly the message is <u>crowded out</u> by the <u>worries of this life</u>, <u>the lure of wealth</u>, and <u>the desire for other things</u>, so no fruit is produced."*
>
> MARK 4:18-29

Jesus said that "things" crowd out the Word of God. The Greek meaning is "to choke or suffocate the divine word sown in the mind." God-seeds can't take root and grow where there are worldly weeds of distractions!

Distractions break down intimacy with God just like it does with our human relationships. When distractions are cast aside, we are able to foster more intimacy, because we are better listeners and we are truly in the moment. My goal for 2019 is to be "preoccupied" with God. Guess what preoccupied means?

"Engrossed in thought; Distracted."

Wow! Wouldn't that be cool? Distracted with God!!! I'm listening! Let's desire God's best!

> *"Pay close attention to what you hear. The closer you listen, the more understanding you will be given – and you will receive even more. To those who listen to my teachings, more understanding will be given. But for those who are not listening, even what little understanding they have will be taken away from them."*
>
> MARK 4:24-25

"Heavenly Father, I repent for being so distracted by many things. Please forgive me for putting trivial things before You. Lord, I desire for my relationship with You to be priority, with no mixture of mindless information. Help me Holy Spirit to be disciplined and self controlled in my time of prayer, bible study and time with You. I desire to be spiritually healthy and fit for your plans and purposes. Realign my mind. Realign my heart. Realign my desires. Realign my time. Fill me with a fresh love for You! In Jesus' name. Amen"

CHAPTER TWENTY NINE

Heavenly Repellent

What do you consider your weaknesses? Do you see them as holding you back, or keeping you from accomplishing more? Do you compare your life to others with envy or jealousy? Do you think too much about your limitations?

One day I was doing some evaluation thinking and focusing on my weaknesses. Suddenly up out of my heart I heard the Spirit of the Lord say,

"*Your weakness does not repel me, it attracts My Power!*"

Amazing how a word from the Lord can change everything and totally realign my view of my weakness! My mind was seeing my weaknesses as holding me back, or slowing me down. I was seeing limitations and just having to settle for less than my desires. But when I heard the Lord say this, my whole vision changed! My weaknesses were suddenly drawing God's Power into my life and into my circumstance instead of repelling! Not only was there a peace, but I felt such relief that I didn't have to worry about being enough! I AM ENOUGH, when I invite and submit to Him!

At the beginning of this book, we started with repentance and we studied how that word can sound so negative and defeated! But the truth is the word repentance is a freeing word! It draws us to the throne of grace to receive forgiveness, healing, strength and power to move forward! So now I'm asking, would you be willing to look at "weakness" in a different way? I promise if you submit your weakness to God in humility, then you are in the best place to receive His power in your life!

Did you know the Gospel of Jesus Christ is needed because of our weakness? The whole foundation of our needing Jesus as Lord and Savior is based on our weakness to save ourselves! In Romans 8:3, Paul writes,

> *"The law of Moses was unable to save us because of the weakness of our sinful nature. So God did what the law could not do. He sent his own Son in a body like the bodies we sinners have. And in that body God declared an end to sin's control over us*

by giving his Son as a sacrifice for our sins."

ROMANS 8:3

So I'm thinking if God sent His Son to do what I could never do, which is save my soul, then I'm also thinking ANY weakness I have can be taken to God and He can help! Again, He is NOT repelled by my weakness....He draws near to me like a magnet!!! Praise God!

Paul boasted about his weakness because he knew God was all he needed! As remarkable as Paul's resume was, he had weaknesses! He even asked God to take his weaknesses, because he thought it hindered his ministry. Yet the Spirit of the Lord told him no, and told him why. Let's read,

"Three different times I begged the Lord to take it away. Each time he said, 'My grace is all you need. My power works best in weakness.' So now I am glad to boast about my weaknesses, so that the power of Christ can work through me. That's why I take pleasure in my weaknesses, and in the insults, hardships, persecutions, and troubles that I suffer for Christ. For when I am weak, then I am strong."

2 CORINTHIANS 12:8-10

There are a couple of things I love about this passage. First, Paul repeatedly asked...in fact, begged for God to take the weakness. It never hurts to ask!!!! I love that Paul doesn't tell us what his weaknesses are. Scholars have written it was physical, while some say mental. Who cares! I love that he had more than one, and by not telling us, then I'm going to assume I can relate to Paul.

Secondly, the Lord tells him one thing and it changes the whole perspective on those weaknesses! *"My grace is all you need! My power works best in weakness!"* Paul now goes from BEGGING for those weaknesses to go away, to BOASTING in those same weaknesses! REALIGNMENT!!! Paul says he takes "pleasure" in those weaknesses because it strengthens him...he's moving, speaking, thinking and living in God's power rather than human strength!

The writer of Hebrews tells us that other "faith champions"...David, Samuel, Samson and many prophets, were able to do mighty things because of God's grace and power working through them. Hebrews 11:33-34 says,

> *"By faith these people overthrew kingdoms, ruled with justice, and received what God had promised them. They shut the mouths of lions, quenched the flames of fire, and escaped death by the sword. Their weakness was turned to strength. They became strong in battle and put whole armies to flight."*
>
> HEBREWS 11:33-34

This chapter also tells us that unfortunately, "bad things happen to good people." It wasn't because the people were weak; rather they laid down their lives for the cause. The key and common ground for the believer is whether we are putting our faith in God and laying our weakness at His feet. He is there to help us! One of the roles of the Holy Spirit is our Helper.

I love Romans 8:26 and the job of the Holy Spirit,

> *"And the Holy Spirit helps us in our weakness. For example, we don't know what God wants us to pray for. But the Holy Spirit prays for us with groanings that cannot be expressed in words."*
>
> ROMANS 8:26

It's Greek time again, so let's define more of what the word "weakness" means:

In Our Body – "frailty, feebleness of health or sickness"

In Our Soul – "weak in understanding; too weak to do things great and glorious; too weak to restrain corrupt desires or to bear trials and troubles"

Whether we are physically weak due to sickness, or weak in resisting temptation, or weak emotionally from trials and circumstances, we have a Lord who wants us to bring our weaknesses to Him. He wants to REALIGN our perspective to see HIS Grace, Glory and Power in comparison to those weaknesses. Let's start with doing what Paul did...let's stop begging and start praising!

One side note...how do we react to someone else's weakness that may not be ours? If I have a pity-party day, it's OK. If my friend has a pity-party day, I'm like "snap out of it!" or "trust Jesus and be thankful!" Why do I think self-pity looks better on me than them? It is so easy to see someone else's weakness and think we can problem solve. Or we think they should "just do this or just do that." Well, Paul had a remedy for that too! Here are a few scriptures:

> *"Share each other's burdens, and in this way obey the law of Christ. If you think you are too important to help someone, you are only fooling yourself. You are not that important."*
>
> GALATIANS 6:2

> *"Don't look out only for your own interest, but take an interest in others, too."*
>
> PHILIPPIANS 2:4

> *"Love is patient and kind."*
>
> 1 CORINTHIANS 13:4

Weaknesses....when I'm down, please help me up! When you're down, I'll help you up! Teamwork makes the spiritual dream work! Jesus working in the believer is a beautiful thing!

"Lord Jesus, I acknowledge that You are King, Lord, and all Powerful! You laid down Your life and became weak at the cross, but You rose from the dead and conquered death just for me! Nothing is impossible with You! Lord, I boast in my weakness and by faith receive Your Grace and Strength! Holy Spirit, You are my helper! Help me to pray, when I don't know how to pray. Help me stand by faith in my circumstances, when I'm tired and discouraged. Help me experience Your grace and peace when my body is working against me. Help me resist temptation when I'm pulled in ungodly directions. Realign my thoughts and help me see my weaknesses drawing me into Your presence. Also, help me not minimize someone else's weakness. Let me be patience and kind and be a friend. I love you Lord! In Jesus' Name, AMEN."

CHAPTER THIRTY

Realignment Lightning Round

I have a sister in Christ who is half my age, yet double my wisdom! Her walk with Jesus is so mature. She yields to Him unlike anyone I know. Her profession is an RN at a prestigious research and trauma hospital, which means she sees life and death situations on a daily basis. My mind can't even imagine what she interacts with and how on earth to handle it emotionally, mentally, or physically. Gosh, I have so much respect and admiration for nurses! Spending time listening to her is always time needed and well spent. She's a gifted realigner! God gives her the ability to confront, yet be gentle. Direct, yet not push. To give warning, yet stand by your side. One of her spiritual callings is to teach others how to grow closer to the Lord. She reminds me so much of the personality of the Apostle Paul. He was the best teacher, because he spoke truth, constantly encouraged and loved the Body of Christ with all his heart. Paul invested himself in people…and so does my friend. This scripture sums it up,

> *"So we tell others about Christ, warning everyone and teaching everyone with all the wisdom God has given us. We want to present them to God, perfect in their relationship to Christ. That's why I work and struggle so hard, depending on Christ's mighty power that works within me."*
>
> COLOSSIANS 1:28-29

My friend and I hadn't seen each other in a few months, so I was excited to have coffee and catch up! Before she came over to my house, I prayed that our time would be sweet and we would have a great time sharing. The Lord quickened in my heart and said, "You're going to ask her questions."

Well OK, I was thinking like "20 Questions" and hoping she wouldn't mind. Then He gave me the questions to ask. Funny thing was, when she sat down and I told her what I thought I had heard from the Lord, she said, "That's cool, because I felt the same thing."

Side note: Don't be afraid to step out in faith if you think the Lord is leading you in a direction. If you are right, He's in the middle of it. If you are wrong, so what? Practicing hearing the Lord, well, takes practice! Ask the Holy Spirit to help and don't get all paranoid about responding to promptings! It still makes me a little nervous to step out in faith with what I feel like He's showing me, but that's part of the God Journey!!!

Back to coffee time and the lightning round of questions. I'm going to do my best to tell you the question I asked and her response. I didn't record or write the answers down word for word, so I'm relying on the Lord! One, two or all may help you realign! You may not totally agree with the answers. That's OK! They helped me, encouraged me and realigned me. Either way, enjoy!

What have you learned being so close to death situations?

"Know your limitations and where you need to press into God. You are not called to everything! Sometimes you have to step back and pray about what you are called to and what you are not. In really hard situations where I have seen death, it reminds me how dependant I am on God, and while I am truly with limitations... He is limitless!"

How do you stay close to God?

"I continuously understand more and more the power of the spoken Word of God. I am more deliberate about speaking scripture

out loud. I have always tried to stay fit and exercise, but this summer I'm also focusing on spiritual fitness. To take more time soaking in God's presence and scripture. Stealing quiet moments to just sit still with God and by faith believe He's working on me in those moments. It matters, because I'm different in handling a day of trauma at work when I've spent time with the Lord."

What God-advice would you give someone your age? (Millennial to 30ish)

"Do hard and holy things! I believe my generation needs to push ourselves in a more deliberate way to the things of God. We tend to either underestimate our strength in the Lord, or we get lazy. If we will run after God, with all passion and desire, He's got great things for us! We need to stir up passion by being in fellowship with others who are also passionate for Jesus!"

What God-advice would you give someone my age? (Say 45 and up :))

"Hmm, let me think. I sometimes see a disconnect with this age. If you look at God as, The God Who Was, The God Who Is, and The God Who Is To Come…I see your generation stuck in The God Who Was OR The God Who Is To Come, instead of pressing into The God Who Is. For example, they talk about what God DID, which is great, but never share what He is doing in the present in their lives. Or they talk about what God is GOING to do or what they are believing God for, yet not seeing or believing God in the *present day. Sometimes they either have a Fear of Hope, or a Fear of Regret, and they like to keep it hidden. In fact, they have a fear of placing a name to it and just naming it out loud. I just wonder what freedoms your generation would experience if they stopped hiding their hopes and fears...named it...spoke it out loud, and then lived daily expecting God to show up. My generation needs you."*

What's your "word" this year?
"Actually I have three words; invest, endure and feedback. Each one of these comes with what I call the 'Second Yes' to God."
Me: What do mean by "Second Yes?"
"There is always a "First Yes" and it is a yes to following Jesus, accepting His gift of salvation, and starting on a path of living for Him. It's a great place, but it's not a part of the "hard and holy" place. The "Second Yes" to God is different. There's power and sacrifice in the "Second Yes." In this yes, the walk with God becomes weightier and you have to count the cost. You are asked to lay down something, and there are choices to make. For example, you have to choose character over comfort. It's the place of decision when you want what He wants, rather than what you want. With the "Second Yes," you have a clear picture of what He's calling you to. With this comes investing more of your mind, will and emotions. There will be times of enduring, which can be uncomfortable and challenging. But with this is the beauty of feedback, where you allow others to speak into your life, as well as you are called to speak into the lives of others. Those living in the "Second Yes" grow spiritually strong

because of the feedback relationship with others who walk in the "Second Yes." This journey has stretched me more than I knew I could be, yet I have seen God do miraculous things in and through me, as well as in and through others. I've experienced how large He is and how small I am. He's so mighty and powerful, yet sees my every need, desire and dream. He's all Lord and King, yet all Father and Friend. Nothing compares."

Coffee time with my friend was stretching, challenging and humbling for me. It was a good reminder that God always calls us to a "Second Yes" or in other words, He continuously calls us to MORE. Why? It's in the MORE that we cooperate with transformation and dying to self. It's in the MORE we become MORE like Jesus. But isn't that what we want? MORE of Him and LESS of us?

Some of you will remember from high school days having to write an essay or give an oral report on an assigned book in English class. I remember hoping to get a classic novel, because there was a good chance you could find Cliffs Notes. This was supplemental material designed to enhance, help explain, or bring more interest to the novel. But of course, in high school you try to take as many shortcuts to totally get out of reading the book! It seems like a good idea at the time, yet when the teacher begins to quiz you on certain details, you realize you're lacking the whole essence of the book. Just reading the Cliffs Notes robbed you of absorbing, both mentally and emotionally, a great classic novel.

Devotionals, bible studies, Christian books, podcast, etc. are ALL awesome for growth as a Christian. But they are intended to be supplements to reading the Bible and spending time with God. It's the Bible reading and time with God that we experience...mentally, emotionally and spiritually, the MORE. We can't be Cliffs Notes Christians. The MORE is in our relationship with Jesus...THEN the people, materials, opportunities, books, etc. help us grow in the MORE.

The definition of MORE is "a greater or additional amount or degree." As we walk with Jesus, we have the opportunity to ALWAYS walk in the "greater" and the "additional amount." Such an exciting journey...the journey that never ends! Let's pray,

"Lord Jesus, help me to not get too comfortable in my walk with You. Realign me to press, push and desire MORE!!! Help me see a bigger picture, yet trust You even in the smallest details. Lord, send me people who are great at realigning when I become stagnant or afraid. Thank You Lord that there's always MORE in a relationship with You! In Jesus' name, AMEN!"

SECTION SIX

Would You Be Willing To Be Restored?

We are now on the final section. For the first five sections, Repentance, Receiving, Reclaiming, Rejoicing and Realigning, we choose to participate in doing our part in our relationship with God, therefore cooperating with God. We can apply each one of these principles and walk in a greater awareness and application. We work on doing our part in being obedient and yielding to God. We do what we know to do, then by faith we trust and let God be God.

In this final section we will talk about Restoration. How do we Restore ourselves from our past and transform ourselves to be more like Jesus? Well…guess what? We don't!

We grow in trust, faith and continuously receive God's love in our relationship with Him. We choose to study and confess scripture. We choose to worship, pray and have a thankful heart. Yet when it comes to restoring anything...it's ALL what God does! He is the Restorer of the broken hearted, the sinful person, the lost, the hurting, etc. The great news is, He is 100% in the business of RESTORATION... 24/7. It's a job that only He can do, therefore He is the ONLY one who can receive the glory!

Yes, we partner with God to speak faith in each other's lives. We serve, pray for others, forgive, encourage and believe that God can do all things. Yet the component of pure restoration in our soul and in our lives is a God-job.

I can't restore a broken relationship...can you? I can't restore someone's faith in God...can you? I can't cleanse a person of sins...can you? Oh sure, our part is to lead a person in the right direction, stand in faith with them, share our testimony and lift them up in prayer.... but God has to show up! It is a supernatural restoration of the heart and mind, which He created. He's the ONLY one who can properly and eternally RESTORE.

Have you ever ministered to someone and their past, their situation, their mental state or their problems were so overwhelming that you thought, "Oh God, I am so underqualified to help them...can you send someone else?" I'm talking about times when you are trying to help a life in such a mess that all you can pray is, "Jesus help!"

In fact, maybe that has been YOUR life...or your life now! A place where you know it is going to take a God-size miracle! There are many degrees of healing and deliverance, yet ALL are significant and ALL are possible with God. Has God restored your life? Then you have a powerful testimony to share. Have you experienced His goodness? Share! Has He pulled you out of the pit of a terrible past? Pay it forward and testify!

God uses our lives and our God-stories as a part of the restoration plan for others. Hearing our testimonies can produce hope and faith in others, which positions them to experience their own restoration with God. I love to read the stories of people in the Bible and learn from them, because in the Word we read about some pretty extreme cases. I know I can confidently say, "God, you saw them, healed them, restored them and loved them...You can do the same for me!"

For this final section, I will share some of my favorite RESTORATION stories. I hope you will be blessed by them. Sometimes it is not even answers we need, but pure HOPE to stay strong and hang on to God! In my experience there have been times I needed an example of how God showed up on the scene and changed everything! The Hope of Restoration can come with hearing a testimony, scriptures you read, time of fellowship, a sermon you hear, or just day-to-day life experiences. He can produce restoration through music, nature, or the appearance of a redbird. In the big things, the small things, in conversation and in silence, the Lord never ceases to reveal truths that only He can reveal. Amazing how His truth and His touch RESTORES!

Let our cry to God be, "RESTORE!"

CHAPTER THIRTY ONE

Bad Day For Pigs

At the end of Chapter 24, we pointed out that Jesus and the disciples were on their way to Gerasenes or some translations say, Gadarenes. At the beginning of the Gospel of Mark, Chapter 5, we read that after Jesus silenced the storm, they arrived at the shore of this region. When Jesus got out of the boat, a demon-possessed man approached him. This man lived in the cemetery for a long time, but on this particular day, he came out from the tombs to seek Jesus. Because he was under the power of evil or unclean spirits, the man wasn't coming to Jesus by his own personal will, but rather it was the evil spirits approaching Jesus.

This man, day and night, screamed and shrieked at the top of his lungs. He was so tormented that he self-inflicted bruises, beatings and cut himself with sharp stones. He was so tormented by these evil spirits on the inside, that he was desperate to set himself free. We don't know how long he was this way, but we do know that the community didn't know how to handle him. They tried to tie him up with chains and shackles, but he ripped them apart like rubber bands. They didn't realize that you can't confront evil by using earthly means or by using human wisdom or logic. No one could handle him, which also meant, no one could save him. He ran from the people, yet was desperate to be free. This man lived alone and isolated, yet was bombarded by unclean spirits on the inside. I would call this a pretty hopeless case.

Yet there was one man he didn't run from, but instead he ran to. It really wasn't the man who recognized Jesus…it was the evil spirits. They knew exactly who He was. And it is interesting what they do at the first sight of Jesus…they bow in worship! Let's read Mark 5:6-7,

> *"When Jesus was still some distance away, the man saw him, ran to meet him, and bowed low before him. With a shriek, he screamed, "Why are you interfering with me, Jesus, Son of the Most High God? In the name of God, I beg you, don't torture me!"*

MARK 5:6-7

Wow! Without any introduction, this man knew Jesus was the Son of Almighty God and he freaked out! It wasn't because he had heard of Jesus, but he knew who He was by the demons. This man screamed and begged Jesus not to torture him! Logically, why would you beg a man to not torture you, unless you knew he was powerful enough to do it? These evil spirits were scared of Jesus! Our kind, loving, compassionate, caring Jesus. I think we forget sometimes that we serve a Jesus who is all powerful. He's a conquering King...The King of Kings and the Lord of Lords! A God so majestic that the demons are terrified of Him!

Jesus didn't mess around. In fact, I believe His purpose in coming to shore was to set this man free. While this man was begging, Jesus was already telling the demons to get out of him! We don't know how many demons this man had occupying his soul, but when Jesus asked the demon's name, it said "Legion." In the Greek, this term refers to "a body of soldiers." In the natural, a legion of soldiers would be about 6,000 men. Can you imagine this man possibly filled with 6,000 evil spirits? And every last one of them petrified of Jesus! And every last one of them OBEYS Jesus! The demons leave the man and enter into about 2,000 pigs, and with Jesus' permission, the pigs rush into the lake and drown in the water!

Word got back to the folks in town pretty quick, and the people came to see what happened. Instead of seeing a naked, tormented, demon-possessed man, they found a peaceful, clothed, calm man with a sound mind. You would think the townspeople celebrated and praised God for the miracle and for making this man whole again. But they didn't. Instead, they asked Jesus to leave. And do you know what Jesus did? He turns and leaves! He will not stay where He is not welcomed. They were more concerned that a herd of pigs were lost that day, than a man being made whole again. They missed an amazing miracle because of their fears, stubbornness, and hard hearts. Gerasenes, a town of people dead in spirit, stubborn, prideful, closed-minded, and full of fear. That is actually as sad as one demon-possessed man. Jesus exercised His power over evil and set a demon-possessed man free, but He chose to walk away from people with this kind of character.

Jesus didn't offer up a parable or share a teaching. He didn't ask to pray for them. He didn't try to explain the miracle and the reality of evil in the world. He simply turned around and walked away. Humbling isn't it?

He did leave them with one thing…a free man. You know what breaks my heart every time I read this story? As Jesus turns to leave, this man begs to go with him. The Greek meaning is more than this man just asking or requesting to go with Jesus. No, the more accurate picture is this man begged over and over and over. I visualize this man on his knees, with tears rolling down his face and arms reaching out. I wonder if he sounded something like this,

"Jesus, please...please Jesus, take me with you. You're all I have! You're the only one who has loved me! Please Jesus, don't leave me here! I'll go anywhere with You! Please Lord, please."

Personally, I would have said, "Well, of course you can come...I wouldn't stay with these faithless townspeople either!" But Jesus knew the big picture. He knew this town needed a miracle walking the streets. He knew He could trust this free man to witness and bring new life and stir fresh faith in the people.

> "But Jesus said, 'No, go home to your family, and tell them everything the Lord has done for you and how merciful he has been.'" So the man started off to visit the Ten Towns of that region and began to proclaim the great things Jesus had done for him; and everyone was amazed at what he told them."
>
> MARK 5:19-20

Staying and witnessing to the people wasn't the choice of this man, but it was the Lord's choice. Have you ever experienced a time when you begged Jesus for your life to go in the direction you wanted because, certainly, it would be easier, feel better and more peaceful...or so you think. Sometimes it's tempting to ask or wish for a life like someone else, because they seem to have it easier and appear happier. Or maybe if you have past regrets, it never seems like moving forward will make things better. Is it hard to humble yourself to God and say, "I trust YOUR plan for my life?" Are we so focused on ourselves and the way life is, that we stop believing that we serve a God who can RESTORE? He is incredibly powerful…at least the demons think so.

There are times when God's plan isn't the route we would naturally take. We don't understand and sometimes it just doesn't make any sense to us. Yet over time, when we look at the big picture, we realize God knew best. We see He can use us to help RESTORE others. By sharing our testimony He can RESTORE one, two, or maybe a whole town.

There's a phrase used so many times when we hear or read about people who have experienced RESTORATION or some kind of break-through in their lives. This phrase has been said so much that to a cynical or negative person, it can be downright annoying, yet to a humble, faith-filled person with their sights on Jesus…it can be a phrase of hope.

"If it can happen to me, it can happen to you."

God is in the business of RESTORING, but what is the condition of our heart to receive? Why did Jesus take the time to cross that lake? Why did that unexpected storm come on His way? Maybe, just maybe, in the midst of evil spirits screaming in this man's head, he prayed, "God help me!" Maybe the cry of his humble, helpless heart made it to Jesus' ears. Maybe.

I know one thing; I don't want my heart, my mind, and my ways to compel Jesus to turn and leave. I wonder what He would have done if the people had said, "Please Jesus, stay in our town and help us. Teach us how to pray, help us have faith, show us how to worship...and we will follow YOU!" He tends to stay where He is welcomed.

> "O Lord, how long will you forget me? Forever? How long will you look the other way? How long must I struggle with anguish in my soul, with sorrow in my heart every day? How long will my enemy have the upper hand? Turn and answer me, O Lord my God! RESTORE, the sparkle to my eyes, or I will die. Don't let my enemies gloat, saying, "We have defeated him!" Don't let them rejoice at my downfall. But I trust in your unfailing love. I will rejoice because you have rescued me. I will sing to the Lord because He is good to me!"
>
> PSALM 13

> "I waited patiently for the Lord to help me, and he turned to me and heard my cry. He lifted me out of the pit of despair, out of the mud and the mire. He set my feet on solid ground and steadied me as I walked along. He has given me a new song to sing, a hymn of

praise to our God. Many will see what he has done and be amazed. They will put their trust in the Lord."

PSALM 40:1-3

"Lord Jesus, restore me! Let every detail of my life be for Your glory and give me the courage to share and witness. Let my heart always be open to more and more restoration in my emotions, spirit and mind. I always want to welcome You in every detail of my life. Restore my life from past hurts. Restore and heal the hardness of my heart caused from past pain. Restore and make my life new and reflect You! AMEN!"

CHAPTER THIRTY TWO

When Jesus Stands

When I was in my early twenties, I worked as a secretary at a local bank. All day long I would be up and down, making copies of documents, taking paperwork to a loan officer, going to the file room or other tasks that required me doing something away from my desk. One day a well-known businessman in the community came into my section of the bank because he had an appointment with one of the officers. When he walked in he acknowledged me and said, "Good morning." I replied "good morning" back to him and told him to have a seat. I asked if he wanted a cup of coffee while he waited, but he kindly declined. After a few minutes

I had to go make copies, so I stood up to make my way to the copy machine in the next room. As I stood up from my chair, this man stood up. It caught me off guard and I wasn't sure what he was doing. I was young, but because my daddy was a gentleman, it didn't take long for me to figure out why he was standing. He stood out of respect for me. When I came back from making copies, he did the same thing. When I walked back into the room he stood up again, then when I sat down, he sat back down. I've never forgotten how I felt… honored, respected, and noticed. This wealthy businessman, who could have chosen to stay seated, stood on my behalf. I knew I would always respect this man for being such a gentleman.

In Acts, Chapter 6 and 7 (read), we meet a man named, Stephen. Because of growth in the community of believers, the disciples decided to add seven men to the leadership and ministry team. Out of these seven godly men, only one is described to us in more detail…Stephen. The writer calls him *"a man full of faith and the Holy Spirit."* Again, in verse 8, we hear more adjectives about Stephen and his faith in action, *"a man full of God's grace and power, performed amazing miracles and signs among the people."* This man had an impeccable reputation and he wasn't just all talk. He was so full of the Holy Spirit that it spilled over into his communication and his actions. He spiritually flowed and over-flowed to others because of his relationship with God.

Oh, to be like Stephen! Stephen had amazing, godly wisdom and was making such a great impact in the community. More and more people were accepting Jesus as Lord and Savior. This religious stir caused a group of Jewish men to start debating Stephen. But they were no match, because Stephen didn't just speak from tradition, religion, or human wisdom. The words that came from his mouth were straight from the Holy Spirit. What a beautiful vessel of God! So what do these angry, resentful, jealous men do? They tell the ultimate lie for a Jewish man to be accused of...they said he cursed Moses and God!

Has that ever happened to you? You were doing "good" for the Lord, yet you were blindsided by lies or accusations. Maybe your intentions were misunderstood, or unexpected strife appeared because of jealousy. Times where you just can't figure out how it happened or how to resolve it. And what can be shocking is it's coming from religious people!

The attack on Stephen was so vicious and the lies were so cunning that he was arrested and brought before the high council. Sometimes it just doesn't make sense when an innocent person is punished for trying to do the right thing to serve God. And do you ever wonder, "Why would God allow it?"

Stephen was in good company though:

- Potiphar's wife lied and said Joseph tried to rape her, because he refused to have an affair with her. He went to prison for years.
- After God anointed David to be King of Israel, he became a refugee and King Saul put out a contract to have him killed.
- Daniel devoted daily prayer to God, yet was thrown in the lion's den for treason.

When Stephen was asked if the accusations were true, he didn't just answer "no." He begins a very long, detailed preaching of the Old Testament and God's story of the Israelites. He knew scripture, but most of all, he knew His God. With every word Stephen spoke and with every scripture he quoted, the atmosphere built and his passion, conviction and righteous anger grew. By the time he wrapped up his speech, he was filled to the brim with righteous anger.

In verse 51, Stephen's passion and anger couldn't be held back any longer. He declared and shouted,

> "You stubborn people! You are heathen at heart and deaf to the truth. Must you forever resist the Holy Spirit?"
>
> ACTS 7:51

He continued with more righteous correction as his voice got louder and louder! It would be similar to standing and yelling at evil judges in a courtroom, who were qualified to decide your sentence.

The evil in these people couldn't take it anymore so they rushed Stephen, dragged him outside the city gates and stoned him to death. Before Stephen dies he even asks God to forgive these people. My goodness, what mercy he extended to them! I remember reading this story for the first time and thinking, "God, that was so unfair and why did you allow it to happen?" Unbelievable.

Then verses 55 and 56 stood out to me,

> *"But Stephen, full of the Holy Spirit, gazed steadily into heaven and saw the glory of God, and he saw Jesus <u>standing</u> in the place of honor at God's right hand. And he told them, 'Look, I see the heavens opened and the Son of Man <u>standing</u> in the place of honor at God's right hand!'"*
>
> ACTS 7:55-56

Can we backtrack for just a minute and read a few scriptures? Each of these scriptures has something in common. Each one tells us Jesus' position in heaven:

> *"This is the same mighty power that raised Christ from the dead and <u>seated</u> him in the place of honor at God's right hand in the heavenly realm."*
>
> EPHESIANS 1:20

> *"Since you have been raised to new life with Christ,
> set your sights on the realities of heaven, where Christ
> <u>sits</u> in the place of honor at God's right hand."*
>
> COLOSSIANS 3:1

> *"…When he had cleansed us from our sins,
> he <u>sat</u> down in the place of honor at the right
> hand of the majestic God in heaven."*
>
> HEBREWS 1:3

Our Jesus, who shed His blood, died on the cross, and rose from the dead, and did a complete work of salvation, then SAT DOWN at the right hand of the Father. Yet, to honor Stephen, HE STANDS!

Can you imagine? Not only seeing the sights of heaven open up, but to see the ONE you have served fully and loved with all your being, STAND on your behalf! I wonder if Stephen even felt the first stone hit his body, or did Jesus just take his spirit quickly! Stephen had done his job and ran his course beautifully. There's a wonderful Psalm that reminds me of Stephen.

> *"Your righteousness, O God, reaches to the highest
> heavens. You have done such wonderful things.
> Who can compare with you, O God? You have*

> *allowed me to suffer much hardship, but you will RESTORE me to life again and lift me up from the depths of the earth. You will RESTORE me to even greater honor and comfort me once again."*
>
> PSALM 71:19-21

When Stephen's eyes locked with Jesus' eyes, his RESTORATION happened. Stephen's body may have perished, but his spirit was 100% RESTORED to his heavenly home. It would be easy to think, "Lord, they needed Stephen...a man full of the Holy Spirit, full of wisdom, and a great leader."

Yet, our ways are not God's ways. God had a bigger plan in mind. Stephen's eternal RESTORATION was about to impact a religious man in such an extreme, radical way, that he would end up writing most of the New Testament. God was about to snatch a Jewish scholar out of the hands of Satan and use him to rock the world for Jesus. At the end of verse 58, in Acts 7, the scripture says,

> *"His accusers took off their coats and laid them at the feet of a young man named Saul."*
>
> ACTS 7:58

This Saul of Tarsus, who proudly watched Stephen die, would become the Apostle Paul...and he would be full of the

Holy Spirit with writings that would supernaturally change the hearts of people for thousands of years to come.

Every person has a different path to walk and course to run. Remember Joseph, David and Daniel? Their RESTORATIONS were unique as well.

- Almighty God redeemed Joseph from prison life and made him second in command of the empire.
- God protected David's life, and made him the mightiest king of Israel.
- God shut the lions' mouths and used Daniel to turn a pagan kingdom toward God.

I love that God is a "big picture God" and He desires for us to see an eternal scale and timeframe. I love that God RESTORED one man by having him step into eternity, and at the same time He begins RESTORING another for a mighty kingdom purpose.

One of the meanings of RESTORATION is "overhaul." Little did Saul know, but Jesus was about to overhaul, reconstruct, and renovate him from top to bottom, inside and out! And aren't we so thankful He did! Saul became the Apostle Paul.

Paul did a lot of bad things before He met Jesus on the road to Damascus, and what is so interesting is he thought he WAS representing God. He was so religious and legalistic, yet he was missing knowing God personally and truly knowing the heart of God. Being religious, apart from a relationship with Jesus, is pointless and can lead us in behaviors opposite of the character of Jesus. Once Paul met Jesus, he shed that religious character and was filled with pure Holy Spirit character. Oh, and he would most definitely need God's power in his life to walk out the challenging path designed just for him.

Paul tells us in 2 Corinthians 11 all about the many trials he experienced, while serving and preaching Jesus. He was whipped, beaten, shipwrecked, imprisoned, and yes...stoned. I wonder if on the day he was stoned, did thoughts and images of Stephen go through his mind? Did he remember Stephen's final words before he died?

> *"Lord Jesus, receive my spirit....Lord,*
> *don't charge them with this sin!"*
>
> ACTS 7:59-60

Paul's ministry was truly extraordinary. When his ministry came to a close and it was time for him to step into eternity, I wonder if Paul looked up to see a young man standing in honor of him...Stephen. What a heavenly reunion for these champions of faith!

No matter what your past was like, believe by faith that you are being RESTORED daily though Jesus. Keep moving forward and leave the regrets, mistakes, and wrong thinking behind. Paul penned it perfectly when he said,

> *"I don't mean to say that I have already achieved these things or that I have already reached perfection. But I press on to possess that perfection for which Christ Jesus first possessed me. No, dear brothers and sisters, I have not achieved it, but I focus on this one thing: Forgetting the past and looking forward to what lies ahead, I press on to reach the end of the race and receive the heavenly prize for which God, through Christ Jesus, is calling us."*
>
> PHILIPPIANS 3:12-14

"Lord Jesus, I am willing to believe that if You can restore the Apostle Paul's life, You can restore mine. I am willing to believe that You can take my wrong actions, terrible words and damaged emotions and turn them into a life transformed and made righteous by Your miracle-working hand. Let the restoration of my life be a light to others who have walked the same path. In Your Powerful Name, AMEN."

CHAPTER THIRTY THREE

Choosing A God Path

Do you remember when you were younger making yourself promises and mapping out your life? I did this at 18-years-old. Here was part of the plan; I would graduate from college, focus on a career, and marry when I turned 25-years-old. Well, that was certainly not God's plan.

I came home for summer break after my freshman year at the University of Tennessee in Knoxville. I was 19-years-old and I remember returning to my hometown and thinking, "this is going to be the most boring summer of my life!" I accepted a summer job at my local bank as a teller and often thought about how many days needed to click off before I could go back to my college life.

One day a tall, handsome man walked in and came to my teller line. My boss introduced me to this wonderful man named, Jeff Graham. After that first introduction, I looked forward to every Friday when he would come by to deposit his check. Of course, I made sure I looked super cute and smiled my prettiest smile.

One Friday he shared that he was having his 25th birthday party at a friend's house, and asked if I would like to come. Jeff says he remembers me acting rather nonchalant at the invitation. I clearly remember thinking to myself, "Heck yeah, I'm going!" To make a long story short, I laid a kiss on him that night, he asked me out on a date, and I was in love!

I did go back to Knoxville for the upcoming fall quarter and I was miserable! Jeff visited me every weekend, which made me more miserable, because I knew on Sunday night, he would leave. My daddy was very concerned that his little girl was unhappy and three hours away from her love. I remember my daddy and mother called me one night and had to listen to my crying and longing heart. It upset my daddy so much that he said, "Now Mary Jo, I won't have you there miserable and missing Jeff. If I have to pick up the phone and call Jim Sasser, I will!!!" OK, Jim Sasser was our local senator at the time. I didn't know anything about transferring to another college, but I was pretty sure we didn't need political involvement or our senator's stamp of approval. My sweet daddy! And yes, I did transfer colleges, got engaged, and became Mrs. Jeff Graham a month after my 21st birthday!

Just when you plan your life to go in one direction, it can turn on a dime, and suddenly you realize you are not just writing YOUR story…you are participating in a GOD STORY.

In The Book of Ruth we read of a beautiful story between a mother and her daughter-in-law. This story is very important because this Moabite woman, Ruth, becomes the great grandmother to King David. God chose Ruth to be in the lineage of David, and of Jesus. But Ruth was not an Israelite and she wasn't Jewish. In fact, she came from a pagan land. How did God help Ruth find her crucial place in history… her God-path? How did Ruth's story become a GOD STORY?

No doubt God uses people in our lives to get us to where He needs us to be and I believe He used Naomi to help Ruth. I believe the influence, wisdom and prayers of an older woman helped line Ruth's life up for an eternal plan to bring about eternal significance. Let's dive into the story and pretend we are there.

Naomi and her husband, Elimelech, lived in Judah, but because of a famine in the land, they migrate to the land of Moab. While in Moab, Naomi's husband dies and she is left as a widow with two sons. She's living in a new land, having to emotionally start over, yet she still has her sons. These two sons marry Moabite women, Ruth and Orpah. For ten years it must have felt like life was a bit better. Although leaving her homeland was hard, she gains the blessing of more family and I'm sure the hopes of also gaining grandchildren. Then suddenly the dream is shattered. Both sons die. Utter devastation. Without the men, there is no covering… financially and spiritually.

As I read about Naomi, I've tried to imagine what she went through. This God-fearing woman was uprooted from her beloved home. Everything familiar in her life… all of her routines, all of her friends…now gone. She is in a foreign land with no husband, no sons…and no means of income. She is left with two daughters-in-law, which is a blessing, yet they have been brought up very different from her culture. Nevertheless, these two girls love Naomi and respect her as their mother-in-law.

Through the talk of the people in Moab, Naomi hears that God is blessing Judah again with provision. This is answered prayer, because now she can return to her homeland. She can return to a place and to familiar people. Now was the time to pack up herself and her only family…two Moabite daughters-in-law. Not really knowing the plan or how to survive as a widow, Naomi begins the journey back to Judah with hope. Then, for some reason Naomi has a change of heart. She now tells the daughters-in-law to go back to Moab. Why all of the sudden in the midst of the journey does she tell them to go back?

Choosing A God Path

As I put myself in her shoes, a few things come to mind. If I were Naomi, I would have had flashbacks of a time I had to leave my hometown, my friends, and everything familiar. I would have recalled the hurt in my heart and the fear of uncertainty of a new home. Naomi must have truly loved these daughters-in-law! She would rather continue the journey alone than make her daughters-in-law go through the emotions of being uprooted. They would be better off going back to Moab and finding husbands. And why should they take care of their mother-in-law when they can go home to their own mother, father and family. Naomi gives these girls a choice.

Naomi blesses them and their future and the three women collapse in each other's arms and weep aloud. What love they had for each other! So much love that these girls cannot bear to be separated from their beloved mother-in-law. She was their family. This older woman loved them with the love of a Heavenly Father. A second time they hug and weep aloud again. A choice had to be made. These two women were spiritually and physically at a crossroad. Orpah chooses to go back to her home and to her gods.

> *"Look, your sister-in-law is going back to her people and her gods. Go back with her."*
>
> RUTH 1:15

Ruth can make the same choice. It is an easy choice. It is a practical choice. And it is such an obvious choice. But it is not the choice for Ruth. Honestly, her choice is more than following her mother-in-law. On this road between Moab and Judah, Ruth chooses God. At this crossroad, Ruth chooses to trust her life to Naomi's God.

> *"Your people will be my people and your God will be my God."*
>
> RUTH 1:16

Ruth has never known anything, but pagan ways and the land of Moab. Now she has made the decision to invest her life to Naomi's God. She doesn't say, "Well, I'll try it your way and with your people, then if it doesn't work out, I'll go back." She is 100% on board...no looking back. Naomi recognizes her commitment. She sees that Ruth is unwavering. This girl is ready in her heart. This girl is determined in her mind. This girl has lined up her will with God. She says "Yes!" to the purposes of God BEFORE she even knows His plan for her life.

I have had the honor and privilege of mentoring young women, who have hearts like Ruth. They have tasted the love of a Heavenly Father and they have made the choice to follow. Oh, they could easily make a 180-degree turn and go back, but they don't. They turn their back to the past, the old idols, past relationships and familiar choices. They say, "Yes, Lord!" and they move forward. Plus they have a testimony and share with other young women!

I have also mentored many who were more like Orpah. Orpah and Ruth grew up the same, with the same false gods and pagan practices. In other words, both were worldly. Both experienced living with a God-fearing mother-in-law and hearing the stories of a faithful God. But when it came to the crossroad of going to Judah with Naomi, or returning to Moab, Orpah turned back. Orpah is not evil, she simply chooses the ways of the world over a God invitation. "Orpahs" truly want the best life possible, but they can't let go of Moab. They would rather live in the familiar, the usual, the wrong habits, the worldly practices, and settle for safe. An "Orpah" girl believes in spirituality, being good and kind, but prefers the pleasures of the world. In fact, she ignores the reality of sin by justifying an acknowledgement of God, yet denying a personal relationship with Him. My heart hurts for the "Orpahs" because you know "Moab" will never satisfy. If you have an "Orpah" in your realm of influence, pray God will deliver her from the "ways of Moab," and instead she will choose a relationship with a living God. Pray she will choose a God-path.

Back to the story of Ruth. As soon as they settled in Judah, Ruth knows they need provision, so she tells Naomi, "I'm going to work and follow behind the harvesters in the field." This girl was searching for favor! I love it! She is fearless and gutsy. She is going out with expectation, with Naomi cheering her on! For a woman to go into a stranger's field could have been dangerous. Women would stand out and be unprotected. Somehow...OK, we know how...God leads Ruth to a field owned by a man named Boaz. He just happens to be a wealthy relative on Naomi's husband's side of the family.

Next, God turns the neck of Boaz towards Ruth. He begins asking the foreman about her, who reveals she is Naomi's Moabite daughter-in-law. Boaz now knows there is a family connection. God spiritually shines a spotlight on Ruth, so Boaz will stay focused on her. He quickly hears and sees for himself that she is working hard from sun up to sun down.

Did you know working hard gets you noticed? Now maybe Ruth had always been this way, but I'd like to think she learned this from watching her mother-in-law. God's favor-light shines on Ruth, and Boaz places her in the field to get the best of grain, abundant water when she is thirsty, and special favor with the other workers. Ruth humbles herself before Boaz, bows before him and pours out her gratitude.

Naomi is overjoyed and can't wait to find out who God has worked through to help her family. To Naomi's surprise and sheer joy, God has used the family covenant redeemer. Naomi tells Ruth to stay close to Boaz's female servants. I believe beyond a shadow of a doubt, Naomi starts praying. You know she's thinking, "what are the odds that of all of the fields, Ruth winds up on Boaz's field!" She sees God's hand all over this and now believes Boaz is who will purchase her husband's land, which will also include marrying Ruth. Naomi did her part to prepare Ruth. Ruth did her part to carry out Naomi's instructions, detail by detail. Plus they wait on God to do His part. And God comes through faithfully! Boaz purchases the land, marries Ruth, and months later she gives birth to a son...Naomi's grandchild. God the Redeemer! God the RESTORER!

When we make individual God choices, one by one, we walk a God-path. Some are easy to make, some are more difficult. And sometimes we need those God-nudges. Orpah thought she chose a "good path" but Ruth chose a "God-path." God choices will always bring RESTORATION. Ruth had no idea that her "God choice" to stay with Naomi would lead her to Boaz! God stories are the best!!

You know what I love most about this story? I love Naomi's friends! Yes, the godly women who had been praying and watching this GOD STORY play out! Chapter 4:14 says,

> "Then the women of the town said to Naomi, 'Praise the Lord, who has now provided a redeemer for your family! May this child be famous in Israel. May he

RESTORE your youth and care for you in your old age. For he is the son of your daughter-in-law who loves you and has been better to you than seven sons!"

RUTH 4:14-15

RESTORATION FOR EVERYONE!

I will exalt you, my God and King, and praise your name forever and ever. I will praise you every day; yes, I will praise you forever. Great is the LORD! He is most worthy of praise! No one can measure his greatness. Let each generation tell its children of your mighty acts; let them proclaim your power. I will meditate on your majestic, glorious splendor and your wonderful miracles. Your awe-inspiring deeds will be on every tongue; I will proclaim your greatness. Everyone will share the story of your wonderful goodness; they will sing with joy about your righteousness.

PSALM 145:1-7

"Heavenly Father, when my life path looks difficult and uncertain, help me stay on YOUR path. Daily, help me to choose You and trust You to lead and guide my life. No matter what my past, my family history, or my heritage looks like, Thank You that through my God choices, You can use my life to be a blessing to others. Through Your grace, mercy and abundant love for me, You can rewrite my future, the future of my family and the future of my children and grandchildren. Thank you Lord, You can start a Godly lineage through me and bring RESTORATION to generations to come! In Jesus' name! AMEN!!"

CHAPTER THIRTY FOUR

He Called Me A "Woman"

At the end of Chapter 7 in the Gospel of Luke, there is a story titled, Jesus Anointed by a Sinful Woman (read Luke 7:36-50). This is a "no named" woman. We don't know much about her, except she is immoral. Yet just that word alone tells us plenty.

Years ago I was asked to perform a one-woman skit, which told the story of this woman. I hesitated to accept until I read a monologue script. The whole script was based on this sinful woman's encounter with Jesus. When I first read it, I cried. This "no name" woman could be any sinful person seeking forgiveness, wholeness and love from Jesus…which I was one. Many times I performed this skit to different women's groups, churches and conferences…and EVERY time I felt such cleansing all the way down to my toes. It ranks as one of the most emotional and yes, therapeutic things I've ever done.

As the story opens, I want you to visualize this scene as if it had been captured on a movie screen. Let this story come alive in your mind and your heart. We begin with a simple dinner party.

One of the Pharisees had asked Jesus over for dinner. This was not just a one-on-one dinner, but other guests were invited too. I suspect the guest list included other Pharisees, as well as perhaps notables. The "who's who" of the town, if you will…your modern day preachers, politicians, bankers, successful businessmen, etc. Also, remember too, there were no women at this dinner party. I would imagine it was a dinner party that was the talk of the town. After all, a certain "immoral woman" had even heard about it.

Let's think about this woman. She is immoral, and everyone in town knows it. I doubt she has many female friends; in fact, she is the kind of woman who is gossiped about and you guard your husband against. What made her immoral and how did her life turn out this way? She wasn't someone who had made just a few bad choices…she was a known, "devout" sinner.

If we step into the scene and interview this woman, what

would she tell us? Would she tell us that perhaps she grew up with an abusive father? Would she say she was uneducated, because she was so poor? Or maybe her choices reflected what was modeled by her mother. We do know one thing; she was an immoral woman who had saved some money. So perhaps she was very profitable at being a sinful woman.

Upon hearing about Jesus coming to the Pharisee's house, this woman makes some decisions. She obviously has heard about Him and probably heard some stories about His ministry. After all, He is going around the city preaching about the Kingdom of God and about changing your ways. And on top of that, He is performing miracles! He raised someone from the dead, healed a paralyzed man and made a man's deformed hand whole again! I would also guess she knows, as do others in the city, that Jesus is NOT a favorite among the Pharisees. I believe that interesting fact alone catches this woman's attention, because she is not a favorite of theirs either. She is an outcast, wicked and evil in their eyes.

Something is changing though in this woman's heart. We don't know how long her heart as been stirring, but we do know she doesn't care who is at the dinner party, or what it will cost her. She is at a place some might describe as, "at the end of her rope." Over the course of the days leading up to this dinner, she may have watched Jesus from a distance. And if she had a chance to meet Him, what would she maybe say?

"I'm sorry Teacher, I never meant for my life to be this way?"

"Please help me, I'll do anything you ask...nobody will help me."

"Is there any hope for someone as sinful as me?"

When we are living a life of sin, we know who we are. Satan makes sure he bombards our thoughts continuously, reminding us of our sin. He also uses others to verbalize how sinful we are. I doubt she liked herself; in fact she probably despised herself. Now she's at a place of decision. What she is about to do is a huge risk, but she would rather take a chance than stay the same.

This immoral woman is coming with a gift. She is bringing such a beautiful gift and it is very expensive. She decides the most precious gift she can bring is a jar of perfume, costing possibly a year's wages. But she just doesn't care. All the money in the world cannot heal her heart, her mind, or her body. She knows this man is special and a man of God...and she wants to bring Him her best.

Now let's start walking into the room. The men are so distracted, that nobody suspects a woman has entered the room. The room is dim...lighted only by candles. She sees Jesus reclining at the table and makes her way towards Him. She keeps her head low. She knows some of these men in a very intimate way and no doubt, they KNOW her. She walks up behind Jesus and stands at His feet. I wonder if at this point if the room went silent!! So silent you could hear a pin drop!

This immoral woman opens the jar, kneels at Jesus' feet and begins weeping. The first tear that falls triggers years and years of held-back tears and suddenly emotions flood like a river. After all, women devoted to a sinful life have learned how to never cry. I imagine that over the years she told herself many times, "don't cry!" When called terrible names in public... "don't cry!" Or when treated as an object of pleasure... "don't cry!" I wonder if she said many times through her pain, "I don't care, and I'll never let myself care about anyone again." Yet because of this one man, Jesus, a flood gate of tears has opened. Now here she is...washing this man's feet with her tears and anointing His feet with perfume.

With every tear that comes from her eyes, healing also comes. She doesn't care anymore who is in the room, except for one man and one man only...Jesus. This woman, who has kissed many lips, now is kissing the feet of the King.

What is interesting is the Pharisees are the ones who question if He really is a prophet, otherwise he would know who was touching Him. Yet, this immoral, sinful woman knows exactly who He is and now she is experiencing Him in full measure.

She overhears Jesus asking who will love more, a person

forgiven a little debt or a person forgiven much. She probably doesn't even care, she just knows what she feels...feelings she has never felt before...Love and Freedom.

Jesus then says something that is staggering, shocking and for this unexpected guest, a word of RESTORATION. He turns to her and says to his host,

"Do you see this <u>woman</u>?"

What? Did she hear correctly? A "woman?" Not a harlot, not a whore, not an outcast, and not a sinner. Not only has He addressed her as an actual person, He then affirms her, while correcting this prestigious bunch...

> *"Look at this woman kneeling here. When I entered your home, you didn't offer me water to wash the dust from my feet, but she has washed them with her tears and wiped them with her hair. You didn't greet me with a kiss, but from the time I first came in, she has not stopped kissing my feet. You neglected the courtesy of olive oil to anoint my head, but she anointed my feet with rare perfume. I tell you, her sins and they are many, have been forgiven, so she has shown me much love."*
>
> LUKE 7:44-47

For the first time in her life, she knows she has done something right...and this Jesus was proud of her. Then Jesus turns to her once more and says,

He Called Me A "Woman"

> *"Your sins are forgiven.... Your faith has saved you; go in peace."*
>
> LUKE 7:48,50

The men in the room argue about "who does he think he is that he goes around forgiving sin." But she knows who He is, and she knows what He now means to her. She just wants to shout from the rooftops, "I'M FREE, I'M FREE!!!" I bet that was a dinner party they would never forget!!!

I can picture her over the next few days. The perfume scent still lingering in her hair and on her hands. She possibly thinks about how kissing a man pales in comparison to kissing the feet of this Jesus. She also knows that a person with ANY background of sin can be forgiven. She understands the power of this man, Jesus, and she just wants to follow Him.

At the beginning of Chapter 8, we read,

> *"Soon afterward Jesus began a tour of the nearby towns and villages, preaching and announcing the Good News about the Kingdom of God. He took his twelve disciples with him, along with <u>some women</u> who had been cured of evil spirits and diseases. Among them were Mary Magdalene, from whom he had cast out seven demons; Joanna, the wife of Chuza, Herod's business manager; Susanna; and <u>many others who were contributing from their own resources</u> to support Jesus and his disciples."*
>
> LUKE 8:1-3

I wonder if this woman was among the women on the tour with Jesus. She may have had more resources than a jar of perfume. I wonder if she and Mary Magdalene bonded quickly. Hey, if she had the courage to walk into the home of a Pharisee, I bet this woman was an asset to the ministry! This woman now looks different, thinks different, speaks different and acts different. She was now fearless, loved, forgiven and FREE!

Thousands of years later, her story is still told. It's not necessary to know her name, because it can be my name, or your name. Have you ever felt that past sins or a past reputation would limit you? Do you ever replay the past over and over, wishing you had made better choices? This woman's past needed extreme RESTORATION and Jesus didn't hesitate, nor did He think she was too far gone! He is ready to RESTORE any past and cleanse any sinful life. So don't hold back! Start walking toward Him. When we humbly seek Him, really seek Him, we will not be turned away. Freedom and RESTORATION awaits!

> *"He restores my soul; He leads me in the paths*
> *of righteousness for His name's sake."*
>
> PSALM 23:3

> *"For the honor of your name, O Lord, forgive my many, many sins. Who are those who fear the Lord? He will show them the path they should choose. They will live in prosperity, and their children will inherit the land. The Lord is a friend to those who fear him. He teaches them his covenant. My eyes are always on the Lord, for he rescues me from the traps of my enemies."*
>
> PSALM 25:11-15

"Lord Jesus, thank you for taking my past, and restoring it to beautiful! Help me see myself the way You see me... free of sin, guilt and shame. Where others have treated me unfairly, help me know that I can trust you. No matter how I lived my life in the past and no matter how sinful I have walked, YOU can and will RESTORE me as I turn and come to You. Just as this woman sat at your feet, I choose to as well, so You can lift me up and restore my soul. Take every part of my past and use it to glorify You! Let my story help someone, who needs to know You and the forgiveness and healing that only You can give. Thank you Lord as you call me by name, it is with an everlasting love! In Jesus' name, AMEN."

CHAPTER THIRTY FIVE

Kissed By God

Years ago I heard a pastor say the phrase "Kissed by God." He was referring to a time in your life when God unexpectedly does something so remarkable and loving that you feel like He's reached down and given you a big kiss! In this chapter, if you don't mind, I'd like to share my personal "Kissed by God" story.

In the last chapter I mentioned that I could relate to the immoral woman in the bible. During my freshman year in college I enjoyed my social life a whole lot more than I enjoyed my academic life. I joined a sorority and filled my social calendar with parties and staying out late, which totally destroyed my GPA. I had a lot of sorority sisters, but only a few I considered close friends, while most were more like acquaintances. I remember one girl in particular, who was a senior and about to graduate. I didn't know her well, but I did know she was a Christian and a "good girl." I also knew she led a bible study. While I was leading a life of sin, she was devoting her time and attention to getting to know Jesus better.

Throughout this college year, I can remember times of crying out to God, because I was scared, confused and felt very alone. Even though I had grown up in church, I had no relationship with Jesus. Nevertheless, I at least knew that God existed and I hoped He would help me. For me, it was a dark year.

Now fast forward 11 years later. I was married to a wonderful man. We had met Jesus and were active in our church and our personal walk with God. We had two beautiful daughters and I was a stay-at-home mom leading a women's bible study in our home. We were learning so much about the Lord and had experienced His forgiveness, grace and mercy in our lives. We were surrounded by amazing Christians who were sowing into our lives, and then we sowed into the lives of others. I was on fire for God and loved learning more and more about Him.

We decided to attend a Christian weekend called Walk to Emmaus, where husbands go one weekend, then two

Kissed By God

weeks later the wives go. It wasn't like a normal retreat getaway, but rather an overwhelming experience of God's grace and love. The weekend centered around fifteen talks, each focusing on a different aspect of God's grace. These talks were given by both clergy and lay (non-clergy) people. Throughout the weekend there were so many special times of just experiencing God's amazing grace through the Body of Christ. At the end of the weekend each person has the opportunity to share with a whole community of others who have been on the "Walk," what the weekend meant to you personally and what you plan on doing with what you had learned. It's one of those God-times you leave feeling filled, refreshed and ready to serve the Lord with gusto! Once you go through the weekend, then you can go back and serve on a team to help others going for the first time on their "Walk to Emmaus."

Now fast forward again 7 more years. I was asked to not only serve on a team, but give one of talks about God's grace. I gladly accepted and couldn't wait to share. I had an outline to follow, then I added and weaved in my personal testimony as it pertained to the topic. I couldn't wait to serve on the weekend and to speak about God's grace.

On the first day of the weekend, as newcomers gathered and we began to get acquainted, I noticed a face that looked very familiar. I really had to dig back in my memory, trying to figure out how I knew her. When she saw me, she walked up and said, "Are you Mary Jo?" I said, "Yes, and I know I know you."

She replied, "I'm Ellyn, from UT...we were in the same sorority." I was excited to see her, yet I also quickly thought, "I wonder what she remembers about me?"

During the course of the weekend, the women attending were divided up into small groups of about 7 or 8 women in each group. Within that small group you easily bond with each other...and by the end of the weekend you have become spiritually intimate with your group of sisters in Christ. Ellyn wasn't in my group, so even though we would briefly chat off and on, we didn't talk very much over the weekend.

On the second day of the weekend, I gave my talk and loved every minute of it. To be able to stand before so many women and testify to what the Lord had done in my life was a wonderful experience. I was a bit nervous, but I knew close friends were praying for me and boy could I feel those prayers. Even though I knew it was me standing up and speaking, without a doubt the Holy Spirit was speaking through me. I watched the faces of women... some wiped tears from their eyes, while others nodded as if to say, "Yes, I can relate." Once I was finished I couldn't wait to thank God for what He had done.

By the end of the weekend everyone was physically and emotionally drained, yet spiritually on a mountain top. On the final day, there was the traditional closing ceremony

Kissed By God

where testimonies were shared by answering the standard questions, "What has the weekend meant to you...and what do you plan to do with it?" Because the weekend was held at a church, the ceremony was in the sanctuary filled with traditional wooden pews. My table of women, that I had spent a weekend of sweet fellowship with, sat on one of the front pews. A microphone stand was centered at the front, so as each woman felt led, she could go up front and share. I was sitting on the end closest to the microphone stand.

About two or three women got up and shared, and then Ellyn stood up and approached the microphone. Here's what she said,

"When my husband came back from his weekend two weeks ago, he came back just overflowing with joy and excitement. It was one of the best weekends of his life. So for the last two weeks, I've been wondering what this weekend would look like for me. You see, I've been a Christian a long time. I've been very active in my Christian walk and especially in Campus Crusade for Christ. When I was in college, I was very active with bible studies. What's interesting is before I came this weekend I was thinking about my college days."

OK, at this point my heart starts to race. I'm not sure where Ellyn is going with this, but all I can do is sit and listen.

"When I was a senior at UT, there was a season where all the Lord wanted me to do was pray. I was used to being active and serving, so being called to only intercede in prayer for others was a discipline. In fact, even though I knew prayer was so important, it

was a season where I felt like God wasn't really using me. Yet I had a burden to pray. Also, I was in a sorority and there was this girl... and she was wild!"

Oh my gosh, surely not! My heart was about to beat out of my chest!

"So I started praying for her...because she was wild!"

OH MY GOSH! She said it again!!! By this time, I could feel myself slide down in the pew. I could feel a heat come over my body, and I'm wondering if I'm going to pass out!

"So before I came this weekend, I was thinking about that period of time 18 years ago, when all God would let me do was just pray for people. I even said prior to coming this weekend, 'Lord, I prayed for a lot of people that year. You know, sometime, I would love to see the fruit of my prayers.'"

The heat over my body turned into tears rolling down my face as she turns to look at me.

"I have a lot of bibles. I have many translations and some I've had for many years. What is interesting is the bible I happened to bring this weekend is the bible I was using 18 years ago at college. This is the bible that I wrote my sorority sister's name in as I prayed for her. I even wrote a scripture by her name. I showed this to the women at my table this weekend."

At this point, I looked back at the women from Ellyn's table, and they are all staring at me with huge grins on their faces. They knew what was coming all along.

"So this weekend, I wasn't sure what God was going to do or

what experience I would have. And while, yes, it's been an amazing weekend... for me, it was more of a confirmation. When I witnessed Mary Jo stand up and testify to what God was doing in her life, I was so blessed. She spoke with such power and joy. At that moment the Lord said in my heart, 'See, there's the fruit of your prayers.'"

I have told this story so many times, and each time I cry. Even typing this now, tears still roll down my face. Now Ellyn and I both have grown children and it's almost two decades down the road, yet thinking back to that weekend never pales. It is always a reminder that when I was at my darkest point, God saw me. He had a plan to RESTORE me. And He loved me so much that He rose up an intercessor to pray for me. Her obedience to prayer changed the course of my life. His orchestration of that weekend was amazing. Ellyn was blessed, the women at her table were blessed, and me...well, I was more than blessed. I was KISSED BY GOD.

> "All praise to God, the Father of our Lord Jesus Christ, who has blessed us with every spiritual blessing in the heavenly realms because we are united with Christ. Even before he made the world, God loved us and chose us in Christ to be holy and without fault in his eyes. God decided in advance to adopt us into his own family by bringing us to himself through Jesus Christ. This is what he wanted to do, and it gave him great pleasure. So we praise God for the glorious grace he has poured out on us

who belong to his dear Son. He is so rich in kindness and grace that he purchased our freedom with the blood of his Son and forgave our sins. He has showered his kindness on us, along with all wisdom and understanding."

EPHESIANS 1:3-8

"Heavenly Father, You look at "time" so differently than we do. You love us so intimately and created us so intricately that You will build on every detail of our lives and use it for Your glory. Help us to anticipate "kisses" from You. Somehow when You "kiss" us, the past can go from a place of torment to a piece of history that brought us closer to You. Although we can't totally understand the "whys," the important part is You are always mindful of exactly where we are. Lord, I pray that You will take every reader's past and turn it into a part of their victory story. Help us lean in and accept Your "kisses." They make it all better.

In Jesus' Name, Amen."

CHAPTER THIRTY SIX

The Big Finale

In the introduction I shared about my friend's mom, Linda. I honestly believe because she prayed for me as a teenager, she was praying me into the Kingdom. Now I realize what a priceless, eternal gift that was. Prayer is so important and when we pray and stand in prayer on behalf of others, their lives change! Especially their eternal life!!!

I can still remember picking up the phone and calling Linda several years after graduation to tell her very special news. It went something like this,

Me - "Hey Linda, this is Mary Jo."

Linda – "Mary Jo!!" (she shouts with joy)

Me – "I just wanted you to know I have met a mutual friend."

Linda – "Who?"

Me – "Jesus!"

To hear her shout, rejoice, cry and praise God was music to my ears! She invested prayer for my life, so I could be restored and have eternal life. And the Lord was sweet enough to let her enjoy the fruit of those prayers. In fact, I know she prayed for all of Lisa's friends. And now over 35 years later, there are five of us who continue to get together and share our lives with each other. We may not have been walking with the Lord in high school, but now we are Sisters in Christ. We each have had different journeys and trials, yet God has asked individually, "Would you be willing?" Our "yes" to God has strengthened us as women, wives, sisters, grandmothers, aunts and friends. Thank you Linda!

In 2005 Linda went home to be with Jesus after years of battling cancer. What a celebration there must have been in heaven that day! The older I get, the more I think about, and even long for heaven. I am relating more and more to Paul when he said,

> *"For I fully expect and hope that I will never be ashamed, but that I will continue to be bold for Christ, as I have been in the past. And I trust that my life will bring honor to Christ, whether I live or die. For to me, living means*

The Big Finale

> *living for Christ, and dying is even better. But if I live, I can do more fruitful work for Christ. So I really don't know which is better. I'm torn between two desires: I long to go and be with Christ, which would be far better for me. But for your sakes, it is better that I continue to live."*
>
> PHILIPPIANS 1:20-24

I look forward to meeting Paul in heaven one day! He didn't hold anything back! He was all in and was so dead to himself and personal desires. There are days when I feel I've learned so much in my relationship with Jesus, but then there are MORE days when I wonder if I even have a clue! Sometimes I find I need to go back to the simple basics of my walk with Jesus. To not complicate things, but instead walk in childlike faith, trust and believe that God loves me so very much that He sent His Son to die for me. Basic principles, yet it continues to bring power, purpose and peace in my life. Never forgetting the big picture of what Jesus has done for me keeps me in the posture of WILLINGNESS!

I also think about when Jesus will return to the earth. Some may say, "Do you really believe that 'Second coming of Christ stuff?'" Well, here's the deal, you can't believe the Bible in parts, or pick and choose. When I made Jesus Lord in my life and Savior of my soul, I had to believe some "far-fetched" things. Like believing in a virgin birth!!! So many times I hear Christians doubt things like the supernatural power of God, the filling of the Holy Spirit, and the return of the Lord, yet they have put their faith in the belief that a young girl had God's child, and He died on a cross for the sin of all people in the earth and was raised from the dead! So really, believing that Jesus is returning to the earth shouldn't be such a faith stretch! If the Bible said it, then it will be a pretty incredible RESTORATION!

I believe many prophesies in the Bible have been and are being fulfilled. I believe we are living in the "last days." Whether "last days" means in the months ahead or hundreds of years in the future, we are all in OUR "last days." I only have so many years to go! If I focus just on this life, it can be kind of scary, disappointing, anxious and concerning. Yet when I focus on my life lived through Jesus Christ, it is exciting, expectant, hopeful, and peaceful…no matter what is going on in the world or my circumstances. I am willing to choose to see things through the Word of God and through my friend and my Lord… Jesus.

This life is quick and as you grow older…quicker!!! Now in my fifties I totally understand the scripture that says life is like a "wisp of vapor" or "puff of smoke." So let's live life in 100% willingness! I am willing…are you willing?

- Would you be willing to repent to God?
- Would you be willing to receive from God?
- Would you be willing to reclaim in the power of God?

The Big Finale

- Would you be willing to rejoice in God?
- Would you be willing to realign back to God?
- Would you be willing to be restored by God?

Let's never give up! Never stop believing! Never stop encouraging each other! And ALWAYS remember the joy of our salvation in Jesus Christ! He paid a high price just to spend eternity with us. He obviously sees us as something special.

In the TV series, AD The Bible Continues, the character, Peter, makes the most profound statement. In this scene, it is a few days after Pentecost, when the Holy Spirit filled the upper room with His presence and poured out His power on the believers. Peter, filled with the Holy Spirit, now knows the path Jesus has called him to. He humbly says something like this, "I'm not afraid of the Roman soldiers, I'm not afraid of the Pharisees...I'm not even afraid of death. What I AM afraid of is I'm not the man Jesus thinks I am."

I can identify with Peter so much! Sometimes I just don't see myself the way Jesus sees me. I easily see my flaws and nothingness, yet Jesus sees more. He sees more in us than we see in ourselves. I am so thankful for that!

As for the final restoration and the return of the Lord, I have chosen NOT to end with scriptures about the second coming of Christ. That's a whole book within itself and there are others more qualified than I am to write about it. I would like to end with a visual I've had in my heart for over 25 years. When I read Matthew 24:36 many years ago, I had a beautiful thought regarding the return of the Lord to the earth one day. This scripture says,

> *"However, no one knows the day or hour when these things will happen, not even the angels in heaven or the Son himself. Only the Father knows."*
>
> MATTHEW 24:36

I picture in my mind God sitting on the throne in heaven. At His right hand I envision Jesus sitting on His throne. Throughout points in time, Jesus turns to the Father and says, "Can I go get them now?"

Father God says, "No, not yet." Over and over, time after time, as the heart of Jesus aches to be joined with His Bride, the Body of Christ, he continues to ask, "Now? Can I go now?"

And again the Father replies, "No Son, not yet."

But one day...one glorious day...the Son is going to ask the Father, "Now? Is it time?"

And the Father is going to smile and say, "Yes, it's time! Go get them!!!"

This is not in scripture, but purely my thoughts on His return. It's a vision that always makes ME smile and cry a little too! But they are excited tears! It may not play out this way, but one thing is for sure…Jesus WILL return! A final RESTORATION will take place! No more sin, no more fears, no more sorrow, no more tears! No more sickness, no more pain! No more earth suits that grows old! No more enemies, no more evil. It's celebration time!

There is a wedding coming soon and WE are the Bride! And Jesus is the Bridegroom! Oh, and as we walk down the aisle to meet Him…oh, His face! Can you see His face? We must be the most stunning Bride ever, because I've never seen a Groom look at a Bride quite like that! What undeniable love! And as He reaches out to take hold of our hand…yes, we clearly see the proof of His passion with His nail-scarred hand. RESTORATION. Praise His Name!!!! Amen!

Acknowledgments

My Sweet Husband, Jeff — Thank you for encouraging me to write another book. You have always been so supportive and you market me better than anyone! I love you so much!

My family — Thank you for loving your mama! You teach me so much about life, love, and Jesus!

Nathan and Terry — To the best team players I know! You not only helped me in this whole process, but you always represent Christ in your words, actions, and your life. You are incredible MVP's!

My Sisters in Christ — We may not be related by birth, but you are my family. Your prayers and encouragement is humbling. Some of you I've known for close to 50 years and some less than a year! I'm still amazed no matter the number of years, when Jesus is in the center, the love and connection is priceless. I love each of you so much!

Jesus — What can I say? Your patience with me is overwhelming and shocking! Let my life continuously live out Psalm 9:1-2!!! You are everything and more!

Hidden Crosses Paintings

Years ago I began painting Crosses for friends and family. It has now become a passion and a full-time business. My work has lots of texture, uniqueness, and hopefully, a piece of fine art that continuously blesses your home with a reminder of God's love for you through the Power of the Cross of Jesus Christ.

Visit **hiddencrosses.com** to check out my story, view my Hidden Crosses Paintings gallery and dealer locations.

Commissions available by contacting me through my website. Follow my work on Instagram **@mjograham**!!!

WHEN HE SENDS REDBIRDS

WALKING THROUGH EMOTIONS AS A CAREGIVER

In 2012, Mary Jo found herself in a sudden caregiving role for her dad. In her book, When He Sends Redbirds, Walking Through Emotions As A Caregiver, Mary Jo takes the reader on a roller coaster ride of emotions, both laughter and tears. Through her journals and raw storytelling, she shares the ups and downs of caregiving. Although every caregiver's journey is different, there is a strong similarity of emotions experienced when taking care of a parent or family member. Past or present caregivers can receive healing and encouragement through her transparent story. Available through your local bookstore or online ordering.

www.ingramcontent.com/pod-product-compliance
Lightning Source LLC
Chambersburg PA
CBHW051347290426
44108CB00015B/1916